THE UNOFFICIAL GUIDE TO PERSONAL FINANCE

FOR TEENS, BY TEENS

WRITTEN BY:
AVANIKO ASOKKUMAR,
SAI BOMMINENI, & ROHIT CHAKKA

COPYRIGHT © 2021 BY AVANIKO ASOKKUMAR; SAI BOMMINENI; ROHIT CHAKKA

Notice of Copyright

All rights reserved. No part of this book may be reproduced in any form by an electronic or mechanical means, including information storage and retrieval systems, without permission in writing from the publisher, except by a reviewer who may quote brief passages in a review.

Printed in the United States of America
First Printing Edition, June 2021
ISBN: 979-8-517452-46-7

Table of Contents

Introduction i

Section 1: Financial Planning
        Chapter 1: Goal Setting 3
        Chapter 2: Budgeting 8

Section 2: Banking, Loaning, and Credit
        Chapter 3: Checking and Savings Accounts 15
        Chapter 4: Credit Cards 22
        Chapter 5: Loans 28
        Chapter 6: Personal Debt 32
        Chapter 7: Paying for College 37

Section 3: Investment Basics
        Chapter 8: Risk vs. Return 43
        Chapter 9: Types of Securities 46
        Chapter 10: How to Invest 51
        Chapter 11: Reading Financial Statements 57

Section 4: Career-Oriented Finance
        Chapter 12: Getting a Job 67
        Chapter 13: Taxes 73
        Chapter 14: Buying a House 82
        Chapter 15: Insurance 86

Section 5: End Game Finance
        Chapter 16: Real Estate 95
        Chapter 17: Social Security and Welfare 99
        Chapter 18: Retirement and Savings Plans 104
        Chapter 19: Estate Planning 107

Section 6: Miscellaneous Topics
        Chapter 20: Starting a Business 113
        Chapter 21: Financial Blunders 116

Glossary 122

The Unofficial Guide To Personal Finance

Introduction

We've all heard the saying that "money can't buy happiness", but for a moment, think to yourself, is that really true? Would you really want to be working your tail off at a 9-5 job when you're 65 because you never thought to create a retirement account, or would you rather be cruising down the street in your 64'? Just like Eazy-E, we hope you answer with the latter rather than the former. Financial freedom and the ability to do things you love doesn't just come by chance, nor is it simply a right that is granted to you when you hit a certain age. Rather, it takes thoughtful and careful planning to understand and lay down the building blocks of your future financial life.

Now we understand this may sound like a daunting task, and it definitely can be, but we wrote this book to address that very issue. Many teenagers such as yourself find themselves extremely confused and frightened by finance; according to the National Financial Educators Council, more than two-fifths of teenagers in the United States weren't financially prepared going into adulthood.

We ourselves were in the very same position. At the beginning of high school, the three of us barely knew the difference between a debit and a credit card. We felt incredibly overwhelmed when thinking about how we were going to learn all of that information while getting ourselves through high school. However, just like any other phobia, the best thing you can do is confront it head-on by educating yourself and understanding this new frontier. Hopefully, you are ready to delve into this experience and are able to enjoy the journey to financial freedom.

While personal finance is often grossly simplified by the school curriculum and many external sources, it requires a fair bit of nuance and know-how to truly navigate it. In this guide, we split the subject into six overarching sections: Financial Planning; Banking, Loaning and Credit; Investment Basics; Career-Oriented Finance; End Game Finance; and Miscellaneous Topics. This book is not a step-by-step guide into what specific decisions you should make in your life. It is not a manual to becoming a millionaire. It is a tool that you can use to leverage your current time against your future responsibilities. It can be hard to figure out how filing taxes work when you are still learning how to live by yourself, so by educating yourself now, you lessen the stress later.

Now, obviously learning about something and actually doing something are two completely different things, but we hope that you can get the most knowledge from this book before you go out into the real world. The good thing is that you've already taken the first step: being financially curious. Just by reading this book and having the willingness to learn about finance means you have started on the path to financial freedom. We encourage you to supplement this education with curiosity in the outside world.

Sit with your parents when they are doing their taxes, watch how they write and send checks, and ask them about what kinds of insurance plans your family has. By learning as much as you can about personal finance now, through both reading and observing, you'll be a much more prepared adult.

One thing to be aware of is that most of this stuff is not fun. We can tell you right now, that no sane person would be excited about filing a W-4 form, it's just the truth, but the benefits you can reap from proper financial practices are worth the boredom and pain. At the end of the day, a well-developed financial foundation is the one thing that you can look to for stability, no matter what other issues transpire in your life. It is critical that you build it up and strengthen it now as you never know what's coming. You can never tell when the next pandemic may occur, when the stock market will crash, or when you'll get into a car accident and not be able to work. However, while you may not be omniscient, a financial lifeline will ensure you have one less thing to worry about in all these situations.

SECTION 1:
FINANCIAL PLANNING

The purpose of this book is to provide you with the skills and knowledge to be able to successfully manage your finances. While that may sound like a daunting task, we are going to walk you through the process in small steps.

Before you understand how to properly manage money, you're going to need to answer two questions: what do you want to do with your finances and what are your finances like right now. Through this chapter, we'll help you answer those two questions and set you on the path to achieving financial freedom.

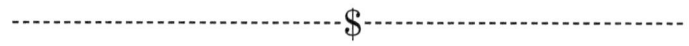

Chapter 1
Goal Setting

The first step to accomplishing anything, whether it's becoming the next Michael Jordan or the next Bill Gates, is setting a goal. Unfortunately, most people go into the financial world without having any clear target in mind. Luckily, we're here to guide you through the process of reaching a state of financial freedom in your life, through financial education. Before diving into any of the nitty-gritty details, you have to set a goal.

Goal-setting is the foundation of your financial success, and it both motivates you and aids in the creation of your ideal financial life. By going through our eight steps of goal setting, we hope that you'll be able to come up with a realistic outline as to what you can achieve with your finances.

Financial objectives, goals you set for how to save and spend money, allow you to accumulate wealth in the long run, and pay off current debt. Specifically, there are two main types of financial goals: short-term and long-term goals.

Short-term goals are those that occur over a short period of time and such targets can vary from a few weeks to even half a year. These may include buying a new car or paying off a small amount of debt. Long-term financial goals, on the other hand, require longer periods, from several years to maybe even many decades. This can include saving up for retirement, paying off a mortgage, or even paying for your child's education.

In order to set your goal, you must follow these eight steps:

1. ***Determine the Time Frame***
   The first thing you are going to have to do when goal setting is to determine whether you want to set a short-term or long-term goal.

   When doing that, ask yourself the following questions:

- Do you need immediate returns?
- Does immediate progress matter to you?

If your answers were yes, then you are looking for a short-term goal, which can offer immediate short-term gains.

However, if you answered no to those questions, a slower-paced long-term goal might be better suited for you.

After you ask yourself these questions and think more about what kind of goal you want, the next thing you want to do is draw a baseline.

2. *Draw a Baseline*

You're not going to be able to get a 20% return on investment within a week or earn $1,000,000 at an entry-level job no matter how hard you might work. Contrary to what your elementary school teacher might have said, the cliche to "reach for the stars" doesn't always work. Setting goals that are way beyond your reach only sets you up for failure.

Use real numbers from your life such as your account balance, salary, and credit score to determine what you can do within your time frame, where the process is challenging, but still within the realm of possibility.

3. *Consider External Factors*

To create a goal that is realistic and achievable, you have to take external factors into account, such as the state of the economy, the condition of the stock market, or changing economic policy. Each of these factors affects the overall economy on a large scale, and as a result, affects your financial matters.

With that being said, keep in mind what external factors are: they are factors out of your control, so be ready for change. To create a smart financial strategy, it's essential to adapt to rather than ignore these factors. For example, if in the middle of your financial goal, the country falls into a recession, you can't simply continue with what you decided on before and expect to see similar results; you must be flexible with your goals.

4. *Plan It Out*

Rather than just going into your goal blindly, make sure you have some kind of process set up so that you have a concrete way of working towards your goal.

Imagine one of your teachers gives you an assignment with no instructions and expects you to finish it by the end of the week. Without knowing what your teacher wants and the specific directions that precede the completion, you would probably feel frustrated and hopeless. The same goes for goal-setting: without the steps to get there, a goal can seem like a hazy general statement, one that is nearly impossible to reach.

5. *Physically Write It Down*

Research shows that writing down goals significantly improves your chances of achieving them.

Why? That's because having something physical and tangible reminds you every day of what you're working towards. There are going to be times when you just aren't feeling it, but when you look at a physical object stating your goal, you will remember the final objective you are aiming for.

6. *Monitor Progress*

Throughout the time frame, actively monitor where you are in terms of achieving your objective. It might seem tempting to wait until the end of your time frame to see how you did, but this won't get you the results you want. As you continue, you should make sure to compare your progress to your final goal and make small adjustments on the go. This will keep you from wasting time.

7. *Measure Your Success*

At the beginning of this process, we mentioned that your goal should have a clear and specific time of completion. When the time period you set for your goal is up, you should objectively evaluate the extent to which you met your goal. The point of having financial goals is so you can achieve those specific accomplishments. However, let's say you didn't meet your goal. That's O.K. The goals you set are meant to be challenging, not trivial, so don't beat yourself up over failing to achieve them.

8. *Learn and Repeat*

No matter how badly you failed to reach your goal, or how far you surpassed it, make sure you learn from it. Albert Einstein once said that "insanity is doing the same thing over and over again and expecting different results". After you complete your goal, if you aren't satisfied with your progress, you should make sure to change certain aspects like your investment strategy or budgeting choices. The biggest blunder you can make isn't losing money, it's not learning from your past mistakes.

You will have to periodically review your progress to see if you are successful or not. You must look back to address the specific problems that you may have encountered that stopped you from achieving your aim. This reflection period will help you ensure you won't repeat the same mistakes in the future.

Prioritizing Goals

It can be difficult to decide what to concentrate on first, with so many overlapping financial goals. To achieve financial success, prioritizing is crucial and necessary. You should start by looking at immediate challenges like debt or emergencies that you might be experiencing and address those first.

A great example of this comes from the history of billionaire Warren Buffet and his former airline pilot Mark Flint. When asked what his top 25 goals were, Flint quickly jotted them down. Afterward, Buffet asked Flint to select his top 5 goals and told him to abandon the other 20. While this may have seemed limiting, it allowed Flint to siphon his energy and efforts into following his goals properly. Having a few specific goals, with real plans, time frames, and consistent monitoring will push you much closer to achieving your aspirations than being overwhelmed with many vague and distracting goals that may not be important to you. Ultimately, after following this goal-setting advice, Flint launched Visionary Airlines, a Silicon Valley-based airfare service, and is currently thriving as a successful entrepreneur.

Chapter 2
Budgeting

Financial budgeting is the process of predicting and planning incomes and expenses on a short-term and long-term basis. Budgeting ties into what we talked about in the last chapter, which is setting goals into an actionable process.

You're going to want to plan your budget according to how you set your goals.

Income

Budgeting is a way of allocating money that you earned into different categories for either spending or saving. Since budgeting requires some amount of money to be allocated, you need to first find a stable means of earning money.

As a teenager, typically your parents provide for you, but there are still many ways you can earn money by yourself. If you don't have an allowance, try asking your parents to do chores around the house for money. If you have time on the side, consider getting a part-time job. Although they typically don't pay a lot, many businesses employ teenagers.

In the future, when you decide to join the workforce as an adult, you will have a much larger income, but with that also comes expenses that you previously didn't have to worry about. We'll also talk about a special stream of income that comes through investment, in Section II.

Expenses

One of the reasons you may want to get a job as a teenager is to spend money on things like entertainment, food, or clothing. However, as an adult, you will have to spend money on things related to living independently and raising a family; your largest expenses will stem from rent/mortgage, utilities, and transportation.

Specifically, there are two different types of expenses: fixed and variable. A fixed expense is one that will not change and is a set amount of money paid. An example of this is rent.

On the other hand, a variable expense may change and cannot always be predicted earlier. An example of this is your home's electricity bill.

Savings

A key component of your budget is your savings. This is how much money you are willing to put aside now for the future. This can be contributed towards an emergency fund or an investment account, but the point is that you don't spend it now. Typically, everything left over after deducting your expenses from your income is what you put into your savings, but there are different ways to incorporate it into your budget, as we will show you below.

Needs vs. Wants

One of the key aspects of creating a healthy relationship with your expenses is distinguishing between your needs and wants. Needs are things that are critical for your life such as food, water, transportation, and hygiene products. If you can't maintain a decent quality of life without something, it is considered a need. On the other hand, wants are things such as designer clothing, video game consoles, or a high-end laptop. They are things you do not need to maintain a decent quality of life.

If you ever come into a budgeting situation where your expenses are too high, odds are you are spending too much money on your wants. Be cognizant of your wants, and only spend money on them when you can afford to do so.

Types of Budgets

I. *Zero-Based*

The zero-based budgeting model is represented by the following equation: *Income - Expenses = 0*

After collecting your monthly income, you should combine both your intended spending and savings for that month and the net balance of those two should be equal to zero, hence the name. This is a good option for someone who has been budgeting for a while and is experienced.

II. *Pay-Yourself-First*
   This type of budgeting model goes counter to some of the other methods. After calculating your total income, you allocate a certain amount of your budget into your savings based on your financial goals, before you actually put the rest of it into expenses. This way, you meet your savings goals no matter what, and are forced to be prudent about your expenses.

III. *Envelope System*
   An envelope budgeting system prioritizes cash income into various sections of household expenses in separate, physical envelopes. By the end of each month, you will be able to view the specific amount of cash left in each envelope and reflect on how well you stayed on track.

IV. *50/30/20*
   The 50/30/20 budgeting model breaks down your expenses and divides them into three categories: necessary expenses (50%), discretionary expenses (30%), and savings payments (20%). This budget is easy to follow for beginners as you can differentiate your wants from your needs and allocate enough money towards your savings.

Adjusting for Mistakes
   As you go through life, your financial choices will not always be perfect or ideal. You might make financial mistakes that cause you to go against the budgeting guidelines you set.
   When something like this occurs, it's important to first analyze your financial standing and see if this is a systematic cost that you need to address in your budget or a one-time thing you can compensate for by cutting out nonessential expenses such as entertainment. After you consider these factors, it is crucial that you adjust your budget by making cuts such as those listed above to be able to make sure they don't hinder your long-term financial plan.
   Someone who really took advantage of this system of identification and correction is a man by the name of Grant

Sabatier. You may have never heard of him, but through budgeting and spending wisely, Sabatier was able to work his way up from an average salary of $50,000 at 22 to becoming a millionaire at the age of 30. He was able to accomplish this feat by cutting down expenses, reinvesting his money, and adjusting for bad spending after realizing his financial habits weren't setting him up for success. For example, by simply moving from a $1500 apartment to a $700 one, he saved $800 a month, and $28,800 in total. Later, after investing that money, he made $175,000! By repeating this process in other parts of his life, he was able to cement his financial freedom without sacrificing years of his life.

In addition to adjusting for your mistakes, you should also account for unforeseen events. One of the easiest ways of doing so is having an emergency fund that covers 3-6 months of living expenses. You can build this by incorporating a small part of your savings into this fund on a monthly basis.

As you will begin to realize, each of these methods requires careful planning and organization. You must track your spending, and you can do so through three methods: pen and paper, spreadsheet, and financial software. Each of these has its merits, but it's really up to you.

Tracking Spending

There are numerous methods to easily track your spending. Outlined below are three of them.

I. *Traditional Pen and Paper*

This method is pretty straightforward as you physically write down your streams of income and outgoing expenses. To maintain your budget, you need to make sure that your expenses balance out and you are left with a certain percentage of your income that can be saved.

II. *Spreadsheet*

This is very similar to the pen and paper method, however, rather than tracking your spending on paper, you are to do it virtually. While some people may view using technology like this as a hassle, it allows for two benefits. First, you don't have to have any kind of material to worry about like a pen and paper, which allows you to be more diligent about your finances since you can log them anywhere and second, a lot of spreadsheet platforms allow you to generate graphs or analytics which you can use to track the trend of your finances.

III. *Free Online Software*

Although they might have a learning curve, these types of applications are probably the best method of tracking finances available; two great examples are Mint by Intuit and Quicken. Along with allowing you to log your finances conveniently, these applications help formulate possible budgets and financial plans based on your specific financial situation.

On top of this, these software also provide alerts of when bills are due or when your funds are low to give you an extra reminder of actions you need to take. These two things allow you to be more cognizant of your budget and are more likely to lead to extra money in your pocket.

SECTION 2:
BANKING, LOANING, & CREDIT

Paper money exists in our society as an advanced medium of exchange that has replaced the traditional trade and barter system. Rather than trading goods and services directly, we use cash which holds monetary value and can be exchanged for various goods and services. The advantage this has is that it reduces the physical burden of carrying goods and can delay the time of transaction.

However, paper money itself can get difficult to manage, which is why we have more advanced financial systems such as digital accounts that can hold money and accumulate interest. In this section, we will be talking about how modern-day banking functions, the use of credit and loans, as well as more specific instances of how the two affect you in your day-to-day endeavors.

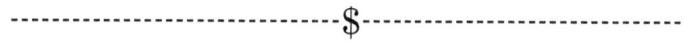

Chapter 3
Checking and Savings Accounts

Before you start navigating the world of advanced finance, you are going to have to understand how to manage and take care of your own money. Two of the most important tools you will need to understand to accomplish this are your checking account and savings account.

From managing your income to making basic payments, your checking account is your fundamental financial lifeline, and understanding how and when to transfer money to your savings account is important to be financially successful.

Checking Accounts

A checking account is a bank account that is used for everyday deposits and withdrawals. There are several ways through which you can transfer money out of your checking account: debit card, check, or a wire transfer.

A debit card is a card that gives you access to money from your checking account. When you buy things using a debit card, money is transferred straight from your checking account to the account you are paying. They can also be used at Automated Teller Machines (ATMs) to withdraw money in the form of cash. With this being said, we highly suggest that you don't use your debit card for making direct payments regularly, mainly for security reasons that we will discuss later.

Another method of payment is through check. We'll go more into detail later in this chapter, but essentially, a check is a physical paper that validates a transfer of money from your checking account to an intended recipient.

A wire transfer is simply a direct transfer of money from one bank account to another. Wire transfers are typically used when it's not possible to send someone a check, or if the sum of money being transferred is significantly large (ex. a down payment on a house).

Savings Accounts

A savings account is a bank account used for the purpose of depositing money and withdrawing funds in order to accumulate interest. Almost all banks, and various credit unions, offer these types of accounts as a way of providing safety over your financial assets.

Savings accounts are a safety net, in that they allow you to set aside money regularly so that when you come across a financial emergency, you don't have to worry about working overtime to make up for it. There will be situations you encounter as an adult that you weren't expecting, like unexpected medical expenses or urgent car repairs, but you can alleviate some or all of the financial pressure through the proper maintenance of a savings account.

Savings accounts are also just a safer place to store your money. Even though savings accounts are not directly accessible, their main function is to protect and house your savings. In fact, the accessibility of checking accounts is what makes them more susceptible to fraud. Although both checking and savings accounts are often insured by the Federal Deposit Insurance Corporation (FDIC), checking accounts are inherently more vulnerable to schemes such as fraud.

You can choose the right checking and savings accounts for you by researching and comparing banks while looking at their interest rates and fees. Like we mentioned before, interest rates on savings accounts are incredibly limited, even the most competitive rates just barely make up for yearly inflation. When looking for the right account, take into consideration your lifestyle and how you will use your account as well. Choose the bank or credit union that suits your needs and gather the necessary information and either open your account online or in-person. While it is possible to hold a checking account and savings account each in a different bank, or even to open multiple accounts, sticking to one bank is often the best practice when starting out.

Checking and Savings Accounts

Comparison	Checking Account	Savings Account
Function	• Used for daily transactions and spending; accessed through banking apps, debit cards, and check	• Used to store money for the long term • Seen as investment with higher interest rates than Checking Accounts, but less ability to access funds
Interest Rates	• 0.04%	• 0.06%
Withdrawals	• Very easy and streamlined to access • No fees or large amounts of bureaucracy to access funds	• Harder to access with more formal process; often comes with withdrawal fees if drawn too many times in a single period (varies by bank)
Common Fees	• Monthly Maintenance Fee - paid to bank for keeping money secure • Overdraft Fee - if you withdraw more than you have you are hit with a penalty • Out of Network Fee - paid when using ATM outside of banks network to get funds	• Monthly Maintenance Fee • Minimum Balance Charge - if you withdraw money past a certain point you will be hit by this fee • Withdrawal Limit Fee - paid if you withdraw too many times in a period (varies by bank)

Fees and Fines

There are many fees that banks make you pay when it comes to maintaining your savings and checking accounts. They're not going to manage your money for free now, are they? You should decide on what bank to open an account with, considering this factor.

Some banks charge a monthly maintenance fee for your accounts, but you can often get around this by keeping a minimum balance in your account. For savings accounts, banks often have a limited number of withdrawals that can be made per month, because of a federal law that limits you to access your savings account less than 6 times. If you go over this limit, they will charge you what's called an excessive use fee.

Although it might seem like a harsh restriction, it also encourages you to budget and save wisely.

One of the biggest traps that debit card users fall into is the overdraft fine. This happens when you attempt to purchase something, with not enough funds in your checking account to cover it. If this amount is relatively small (several hundred dollars) the bank steps in and covers you for your funds, but your checking account goes into the negative, and you are charged an overdraft fine. This part of the system called overdraft protection, which allows you to withdraw past your balance a certain amount, but for a fine per transaction.

Bank Account Security

Managing your money is easy when dealing with small amounts, but once you reach the stage of living on your own and start earning your own income, it can be difficult keeping track of things. This can result in something as minor as having to pay a penalty fee to something as significant as losing thousands of dollars to a criminal.

One of the biggest problems concerning financial security in America is identity theft. This widespread problem affects hundreds of thousands of Americans annually. In case you don't understand what identity theft is (no, it's not somebody literally impersonating you), it is when an individual steals your banking information and makes purchases in your name.

To avoid this problem, keeping your bank account information secure is extremely important. Never give away your Personal Identification Number (PIN), as it gives direct access to your bank account. Additionally, log your purchases and double-check your purchase history to ensure that you were the one behind them. If you see any discrepancies between your purchases and your bank's report, contact your bank immediately; if you need to, lock your accounts. Doing so will keep your money safe, and if any money has been lost, your bank might be able to compensate you for it.

How Do Checks Work?

A check is an order to transfer money from one bank account to another. First, it all starts when the check sender

Checking and Savings Accounts

writes the paper check. The diagram below explains all the different parts that you need to fill out. Then the check is given to the receiver, which can be done through mail, or just in-person. Next, for the money to be transferred, the receiver must go and deposit the check. Nowadays, this procedure has mostly become digital, through taking a picture of the check with your bank's app, but you can also go to a bank directly to deposit it.

Though, there are a few caveats to processing a check. Most checks must be deposited or cashed-in within 6 months of the written date. If a check is held on to longer than this, it will expire.

Additionally, if the person who writes the check doesn't have enough money in his or her account at the time the check is deposited, then the check bounces. This means that the deposited check was bad, and the bank could not complete the transfer.

Whenever a check bounces, both the check writer and depositor have to pay a fine to their respective banks. Writing a bad check is usually done on accident, where the writer doesn't realize there aren't enough funds in their account, so in most cases you can recover the money for the fine as well as the original amount from the check writer. In the case of fraud, however, where one of the parties knows it is a bad check and willingly deposits or writes it, the perpetrator of the fraud can get charged with a crime.

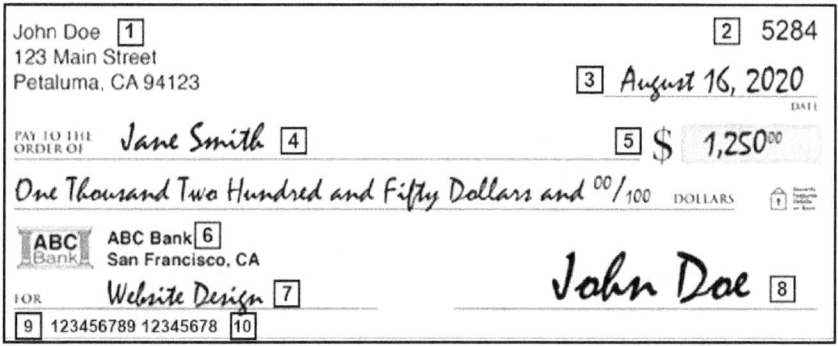

1. Personal information including name and address is located here; personalized checkbooks have this information printed on there by default.

2. Unique check number allows you differentiate between the different checks within an individual checkbook.
3. Date of when the check was written out by the sender to the recipient.
4. Name of the person, company, or entity that is the recipient of the check.
5. Check's dollar amount in numerical form is in the box. On the line below, the dollar amount is written in words. 00/100 represents 0 cents. It is important to write across or draw a line across the whole space in order to prevent tampering.
6. This symbol identifies the bank that provided the checkbook and is printed on every check.
7. This line is meant for the check's purpose, which describes the reason for payment.
8. Check sender's signature which verifies that all of the information is accurate is signed here.
9. The nine-digit number present represents the specific bank that the check is being sent from. This number is unique to each financial institution.
10. This is your eight-digit account number that identifies your payment information. This allows for your respective bank to identify where the money was taken from.

Types of Financial Institutions

I. *Commercial Banks*

These are the most common types of banks, offering services such as granting loans, accepting deposits, and opening checking accounts. These financial institutions generate revenue by providing their customers with loans and charging interest on them. Their funds come from money that is deposited in savings accounts, checking accounts, and Certificates of Deposits (CDs). Examples of these types of banks include prominent "Fortune 500" companies such as Bank of America, Chase Bank, and Wells Fargo.

II. *Credit Unions*
These institutions are similar to banks, but rather than being corporate-operated, they are owned and run by participating members. They offer similar services to that of banks but do so at more competitive rates, as they are non-profit partnerships. Examples include Navy Federal Credit Union, Pentagon Credit Union, and Alliant Credit Union.

III. *Mutual Savings Banks*
These are banking institutions operated by local municipal governments. Members contribute to an overarching common fund from which members can withdraw loans and capital. Examples include Eastern Bank, Dollar Bank, and Liberty Bank.

Chapter 4
Credit Cards

Another advanced form of finance is the idea of credit. Credit, in essence, is the idea of borrowing money with a promise of repaying it in the future. Although the practice of exchanging money directly with goods and services might seem good enough for most economic practices, credit allows people to use time as a buffer and tool to further manipulate capital. Typically, there is some sort of interest associated with this so that the person lending the money gains something out of the interaction.

It is crucial to keep in mind that your financial opportunities are directly related to your credit. For this reason, understanding the rules of credit and how to build and maintain it is extremely important, starting with your credit card.

Credit Cards

A credit card, in essence, is a card that gives you access to a flexible revolving loan, with multiple components to it. A credit card lets you take a certain amount of money out as credit, with the promise to pay all or a portion of it back at the end of the month. The main advantage of using a credit card over a debit card is that rather than directly taking money out of your bank account for each transaction, a credit card allows you to delay all of those payments to the end of the month into one larger bill. However, there are a few stipulations to this.

The maximum amount that you can access from your credit card in a given month without being penalized is your credit limit. It is usually best not to max out your limit because this negatively affects your credit score (we'll get into what a credit score is later). This credit limit usually starts low but can increase if you request a higher limit and are improved.

Where the credit card begins resembling a loan is with the concept of APR. APR stands for Annual Percentage Rate, which is the amount of interest you must pay per year on your outstanding credit card debt. This is usually distributed throughout your monthly payments. For example, if the APR on a certain credit card is 24%, you divide that by 12 months, which would result in a monthly interest rate of 2% on the credit card debt that you have not yet paid back. Notice how we said that it only matters for the debt you have accumulated. If you pay back your borrowed amount in full at the end of the month, there you gain no interest. Similar to APR, APY, or Annual Percentage Yield, measures the effective interest rate that accounts for compound interest.

There are many reasons to take on at least a little bit of credit card debt, one of which is to delay your payments until you have more money. This is where the minimum payment comes in. Since credit card companies and banks want you to go into debt, so that they can collect more interest from you, they allow you to pay a very small portion of the amount you borrowed, without getting fined. Of course, you can pay anywhere between this minimum payment and the full amount without getting fined, but what is best depends on your immediate financial situation.

Choosing a Credit Card

When choosing a credit card, there are many things to consider: APR, fees, loyalty points, and cashback. Oftentimes, a credit card company might entice you to get their credit card, with extremely low or even 0% APR for a small period of time, but this APR will usually increase to their normal rates or even higher after that time period is completed. APR should be carefully considered if you plan to carry a balance. However, if you plan to pay in full each month, this shouldn't worry you too much.

Next, many cards have fees for things such as late payments and annual maintenance. Think about your financial lifestyle and look for cards that minimize the amount of fees and fines you have to pay overall.

If you are looking to get extra rewards for using your credit card often, you should look for a card that has a reliable point system that is optimized for the categories that you tend to spend the most money on. One thing to be careful about, however, is overspending in order to get more loyalty points.

Cashback on credit cards is also similar to a loyalty point system, where credit card providers reward users for spending money using their card, with direct money paid 'back' to them. The rates for cashback are typically from 2% to 5% of the value of monthly expenditure. Most cards provide a flat rate for all purchases, but some have varying cash back percentages based on the type of purchase. Like loyalty cards, these cards may tempt you to spend more money in order to get extra cashback, but keep in mind that you should only spend what you can afford to pay back in the future. Most credit cards also have a cumulative closing date which marks the end of their respective billing period.

Credit Card Fees

Although at some point in your life, you may have learned to just ignore the fine print sections of contracts, when it comes to important financial decisions, like getting a credit card, attention to detail is extremely important. There are many fees that are often disguised and hidden in credit card contracts, which is why many of the deals that credit card companies offer are too good to be true.

When first getting a credit card from a new bank, there is typically an initial setup fee associated with getting and activating the card. Credit cards also have unique annual fees that are charged to consumers for using their cards. An over-the-limit fine is charged when the account balance goes over the set credit limit. Additionally, late payment fees are charged for late or missed payments. If you own multiple cards and are trying to transfer the balance from one card to another, your company will charge 3%-5% on the total transfer amount in the form of a balance transfer fee.

How Do Credit Scores Work?

Credit scores are personalized numbers ranging between 300 to 850 that determine a person's trustworthiness with money based on their previous credit history. Generally, almost all credit scores land between 600-750, and higher scores, of 750 or above, are considered to be top-tier and are the result of a long history of well-made credit decisions. Scores are calculated by organizations known as credit bureaus using information about you from various financial institutions. Credit scores are used by banks, credit card companies, and car dealerships to estimate a person's ability to pay back loans and make monthly payments.

How to Maintain Good Credit

With the right financial habits and enough time, gaining a high credit score is an easy task to accomplish. There are four critical rules you must follow to build and maintain a high credit score.

I. *Never Miss a Payment*

The most important thing to remember regarding credit is to never miss a payment. If you miss payments, your credit will reflect that, and your credit score will consequently decrease. This doesn't mean you have to pay the full amount every time; paying off just the minimum amount will usually ensure that your credit score does not decrease.

II. *Never Max Out Your Credit*

You want to make sure you don't approach your credit limit or the point where you 'max out'. Most experts recommend staying below 30% of your credit limit. As you approach your credit limit, you signal your credit card provider that you may be unable to pay off your bills, which subsequently affects your credibility with other financial institutions.

III. *Check Your Credit Reports*

Although this may seem a bit over the top, many times, credit reports can be filled with inaccuracies that may be affecting your credit score. These errors can be from something as simple as a clerical mistake or as sinister as criminal activity. Make sure that your credit reports reflect *your* spending and not that of an identity thief.

IV. *Limit Credit Card Openings*

Many people have multiple credit cards, typically for different purposes, but opening too many within a short period of time can be a detriment to your credit score. Lenders may see the opening of many new credit cards as an inability to finance things regularly.

Cumulatively, following the four rules above will ensure that your credit will be able to develop and maintain itself. In the long run, keeping a careful watch over your credit will provide you with financial opportunities you may not have had otherwise.

What Is a Credit Report?

A credit report is a summary of the management and repayment of debts in your record. It consists of documents and information specific to your credit activity. Furthermore, it includes the business that provided you with a credit card or loan, an accumulated amount for the loan or the credit history of your card, timeliness of payments, and the amount of the respective payments, as well as any missed payments. This information is used to calculate a large part of your credit score.

Hard Inquires vs. Soft Inquiries

If a lender or a creditor ever asks a credit bureau to view their credit report, an inquiry will be written along with your credit history. This inquiry itself will later get added to your credit report, albeit temporarily, but can affect your future credit opportunities. These inquiries are divided into two categories: hard and soft. A hard inquiry occurs when a lender examines your credit report in order to make a decision; this form of inquiry has the potential to lower your credit score. A soft inquiry, on the other hand, occurs when you check your account or when a credit card company checks it for you. Your credit report will not be impacted in this situation.

Hard inquiries can negatively affect your score for a reason we talked about before: taking on too many new accounts. The act of opening too many new credit cards or taking on too many loans within a small period of time is visible on your credit report.

What Are Credit Bureaus?

Credit bureaus provide you with information on your credit history using the financial documents that are available from them. Typically, a creditor, like your bank, provides financial statements and payment history to credit bureaus. From this, they calculate your credit score. The three biggest and most commonly used credit bureaus are Experian, Equifax, and TransUnion.

The Unofficial Guide To Personal Finance

Chapter 5

Loans

In the previous chapter, we talked about credit cards, which in essence are loans that reset monthly. Now, we are going to discuss conventional loans, which can be used for a large range of purposes.

Before going into this chapter, there are a few important aspects of loans that you should know. A loan is a certain amount of money given to an individual with the expectation of the repayment of that money in the future with additional interest. A loan, like any contract, is always agreed to by both sides. Loans are given out by corporations or financial institutions, upon approval of a request from a customer or client. Loans can generally be categorized into the following: personal, student, auto, home, and commercial. However, for the sake of keeping this book focused on personal finance, we'll be leaving out commercial loans.

A key term you will need to understand as we explore this section is principal; this is simply the money that the loan was originally taken out for and what interest calculated off of.

Personal Loans

A personal loan is any amount of money borrowed for personal needs such as paying off credit card debt, taking a vacation, or even making a large purchase. Utilizing personal loans can be a good way to consolidate the debt of many smaller high-interest loans into a single monthly rate. For personal loans, you must make monthly payments consisting of both the principal and accumulated interest. A term that is key for understanding how these loans differ is collateral.

Collateral is an asset that is offered as a kind of "insurance" for the loan provider so that providers can protect the money they distribute. This is usually necessary when a large amount of money is involved or if you have a poor credit score. If the lender has the right to a certain high-value asset you own, and you decide to run off with the loan money or are unable to pay it back, they can simply seize the collateral asset as compensation.

Generally, there are four main categorizations of personal loans.

I. *Unsecured Personal Loans*

These are loans offered without any collateral. Depending on your credit score, lenders may provide you with these types of loans. By having a high credit score, it is usually easier to get approval for these loans, since it shows that you have high financial credibility. Although, this trust is usually accompanied by higher interest rates since the lender is still taking on some risk by not taking collateral.

II. *Secured Personal Loans*

Unlike unsecured loans, secured loans *are* backed by collateral. Lenders providing these loans choose what asset is to be considered collateral. These loans tend to have lower interest rates than unsecured ones.

III. *Fixed-Rate Loans*

These loans have fixed interest rates and monthly costs, hence the name. This makes it easier to follow a strict budget, without any discrepancies.

IV. *Variable-Rate Loans*

These loans start at an interest rate that can later increase or decrease. There will always be specific limits on the maximum increase or decrease of the interest rate, which means that they will usually start at a lower rate. Of course, the financial institution can't just increase it for no reason; the rate usually mirrors something like an index of the economy.

Open-end and Closed-end Loans

A person has the right to borrow numerous times with an open-ended loan, within the confines of the maximum loan amount. An example of an open-end loan is a credit card because after repaying the existing debt, you can take out more money on credit up until your limit. A credit limit is the largest amount of money that can be lent at a certain time.

For closed-end loans, you may not borrow more money under the same loan once you have paid off some of it. This means the money you take is final. Most general loans are structured this way, so that once the loan principal and interest is completely paid off, the loan is closed. The loan balance decreases as someone processes the non-repayment for the lender.

Student Loans

Student loans are used to pay for educational expenses. These loans are usually closely monitored to make sure that only educational costs are covered. These loans help pay for tuition, room and board, textbooks, and other expenses associated with a college education.

To apply for federal student loans you must use the Free Application for Federal Student Aid (FAFSA®) form, a standardized form that determines amounts you can borrow. The student loans you then receive fall into two categories: Direct Subsidized and Direct Unsubsidized.

I. *Direct Subsidized*

This means the government will pay off your interest for either half the time you're in college, in the six months "grace period" after you graduate, or if you fall behind on your payments. Rates on these loans are 2.75%, and individuals will receive from $23,000 to $65,000.

II. *Direct Unsubsidized*

The interest here is paid by students for the entire duration of their loan. Rates are slightly higher at 2.75% given the fact the student has to shoulder most of the cost making repayment riskier for the lender. Using these loans, individuals can receive anywhere from $8,000 to $73,000 in loans.

Keep in mind that these loans are not mutually exclusive, and you can use a combination of both depending on the amount of aid necessary for up to a maximum of $138,000. Also, even though the aforementioned federal student loans are the most commonly taken student loans, there also exists a world of private student loans.

Mortgage Loans

Mortgage loans or mortgages are a common type of loan used to finance the buying of a house. Houses can be expensive, and it's difficult to pay all that money in one upfront payment, which is why mortgages exist. Homeowners must still pay a small percentage of the house value upfront but can finance the rest through a mortgage. The homeowner basically has full ownership of the house, even before the mortgage is completely paid off.

Most mortgages have either a 15-year or 30-year time period, but some have times in between, and those times don't have to be final. The longer the repayment period, however, the higher interest rates tend to be, as there is more risk for the lender. Mortgages also have fixed and variable interest rates, like personal loans, and work the same way.

Chapter 6
Personal Debt

Debt, in the simplest of terms, is money owed. This can result from a variety of things such as taking out a loan or not paying your bills. When you think of the word debt, you probably think it's something to avoid at all costs (pun intended), but this isn't necessarily true. Before we dive into this chapter, we want to make sure that you understand that debt isn't inherently bad: it can often be beneficial, like when taking on some debt from a loan to support your business ventures. It's important not to stigmatize debt to the point where you never take any of it, as you lose opportunities for growth.

Debt should be thought of as another tool in your toolbox of financial knowledge, not as a burden that is blocking you from financial success. That is not to say you should keep borrowing until you dig yourself into financial ruin, but understanding it and taking on appropriate amounts can help you more than avoiding it will. The key to having a good relationship with debt is knowledge. In this chapter, we will discuss three facets of personal debt so you can get a better understanding of it: the sources of personal debt, how to pay it off, and filing bankruptcy.

Sources of Debt

I. *Consumer Credit*

Consumer credit is issued by banks, distributors, and others to encourage consumers to buy products and pay off the expense with interest over time. There are two types of consumer credit: installment credit and revolving credit. Installment credit allows people to pay for expensive items with equal payments that are spread out over some time. This type of credit has a certain number of fixed payments, whereas revolving credit is to

Personal Debt

be automatically renewed as debt is paid off. Examples of revolving credit include credit cards.

II. *Personal Loans*

A personal loan is a sum of money that you borrow for almost any reason and pay back over several years with interest. This could range from anything from making a car payment to going on vacation. These loans do tend to have higher interest rates, so you might want to be cautious about using them.

III. *Auto Loans*

This is a loan used by an individual to buy a motorized vehicle. Auto loan payments are commonly structured as periodic installments and a car loan is secured against the specific vehicle you want to buy, which ensures that your vehicle acts as collateral for your loan. If you are unable to pay your car loans, your car will be repossessed, but you won't be compensated for any of your past payments.

IV. *Small Business Loans*

This is a type of loan you have a good chance of taking out in the future. Going upwards to a range of about $370,000, these types of loans account for $68 billion of consumer debt. While these kinds of loans aren't inherently risky, as they can be used to kickstart your business, they do involve the risk of adding to your personal debt in the long-term. If you plan on starting a business, make sure you are willing and able to take on the risk before applying for small business loans.

V. *Payday Loans*

These types of loans are one of the biggest contributors to personal debt in the U.S., adding nearly $40 billion to consumer debt each year. These types of loans involve extremely small amounts of cash, usually ranging from $100-$500, but borrowed with high-interest rates. Meant to be a last resort if someone requires immediate cash, these loans are rarely paid off, because, well, the people who take them on are strapped for cash. Although the idea is that you would pay the loan back on the day you get paid (hence, payday loan), the high interest rates associated with them make it difficult to do so.

VI. *Farm Loans*

Truthfully, you will probably never run into these kinds of loans unless you are steadfast in being a farmer or really like horses. However, if you for some reason need one, be aware that these kinds of loans act in similar ways to small business loans with more flexible payment plans and run the economy about $120 billion in consumer debt.

VII. *Residential Mortgage Debt*

These are the largest and the most common forms of debt in America. They stem from mortgage payments and the debt which is undertaken to buy houses and property totaling nearly $11 trillion in debt annually.

How to Pay Off Debt

To pay off your debt, make sure to first define the type of debt you are working with. This could include student loans, credit cards, or even mortgages, and creating a personalized plan for debt payoff can be easier by understanding the specific types of debt you are facing. You should begin by creating a specific budget with personalized categories and see where you can cut down your costs. Then, pay off the debt that is of higher interest first and pay more than the minimum balance, if possible. After that, limit credit card spending and use bonuses and other money given to you towards debt rather than personal items. By doing this, you will be able to effectively and quickly get rid of your debt.

Another option for paying off debt is through consolidation. Debt consolidation combines all of your smaller sources of debt into one larger one. This is usually done by taking out a personal loan to pay off all the existing debt, and then continuing monthly payments on that loan. However, if your debt is too large, taking out a loan might be difficult with poor credit, but there are other solutions.

Personal Bankruptcy/Default

In the U.S. financial system, there are many ways you can get out of debt, one of which is bankruptcy. Although when most people hear the word bankruptcy, they think of businesses shutting down and closing. There is another kind of bankruptcy that can be filed by individuals when they are unable to repay debt, based on certain criteria. Bankruptcy is a tool, but it should be saved as a last resort, as it can stay on your financial record for up to a decade and will negatively affect your credit.

The two main forms of personal bankruptcy are called Chapter 7 Bankruptcy and Chapter 13 Bankruptcy. Although it's not as simple as shouting, "I DECLARE BANKRUPTCY!" like The Office's Michael Scott, the process of filing for bankruptcy is used by many people as a means of freeing themselves from unfulfillable debts.

I. *Chapter 7 Bankruptcy*

Personal bankruptcy is most conventionally thought of as Chapter 7 Bankruptcy. If someone files for Chapter 7 Bankruptcy, they must turn over all liquid assets within their possession. A liquid asset is something of value that can be quickly converted to cash. Though there are some stipulations to this. The government breaks liquid assets into two categories: exempt and non-exempt. Exempt liquid assets are those that cannot be taken from an individual who has filed for bankruptcy. This exists so that bankruptcy filers can continue to live with some of their essential possessions, like a necessary motor vehicle, clothing, or household appliances. Non-exempt assets include everything else the filer has.

II. *Chapter 13 Bankruptcy*

Filing Chapter 13 bankruptcy isn't as extreme as chapter 7, as you still have to pay off your debt, but you arrange a plan to do so over a longer period of time, and it can be a reduced amount. Depending on your circumstances, you might be required to either completely or partially pay off your debts. The way you would do so is by creating a payment plan for your creditors, but a legal hearing must take place with your creditors approving the plan and the judge accepting it as well. Choosing Chapter 13 Bankruptcy might be better for you if you can pay off those debts, and you don't want to lose your rights to certain assets.

Default

Another term you might hear when it comes to debt obligations is default. This is very closely related to bankruptcy, but it is something that is imposed upon you and it is something that you want to avoid at all costs. A default happens when you fall behind on your payments on loans by a certain amount, and it can have devastating effects on your credit score and financial status as a whole.

Repossession

Repossession occurs when a debtor is not able to meet their loan payments, and the creditor claims ownership of the collateral. Typically, a car is the first thing to be repossessed, but there is also a special type of repossession called a foreclosure. A foreclosure occurs when a homeowner fails to pay their mortgage payments, and the mortgage lender repossesses the house.

Chapter 7
Paying For College

Although we previously talked about investing from a purely monetary perspective, there are other forms of investment. College is one such investment towards your future. You might be thinking, "Well, Bill Gates and Steve Jobs dropped out of college, so it must not be that important." Well, sorry to disappoint you, because unless you have a groundbreaking idea on par with Windows or the Macintosh, you won't have the same success as them. Getting a higher education almost always guarantees higher pay when compared to applicants in a similar career.

College Applications
Before you even start college, you have to go through the application process, which can be expensive on its own. Many universities have a certain upfront fee that they expect you to pay just to review your application. This usually ranges from $50-$75, but depending on other factors, such as whether the school is public or private, they may be lower or higher. High school exams, such as Advanced Placement testing and SAT and ACT testing, can be costly, but it is a smart investment for the future. You will set yourself apart from your peers by taking standardized exams and doing well on them. If you are unable to afford tests, you can often apply for a fee waiver. Furthermore, apart from just taking the tests, there are fees associated with sending your tests to college. If you or your family has a low income or are first-generation college students, and you are eligible by meeting the requirements, you can file for fee waivers on your Common Application.

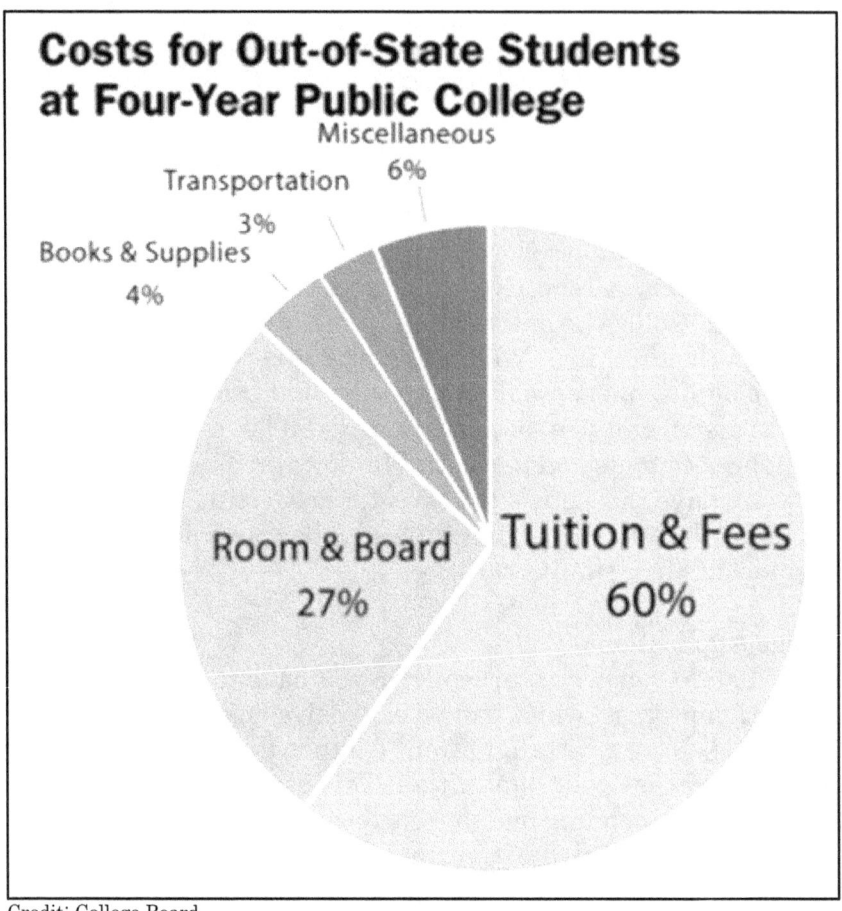

Credit: College Board

Financial Aid
    To help an individual pay for their college experience, financial aid will be given from federal, state, and private organizations. There are two forms of applying for aid: financial need and merit. Need-based aid is given after the federal government reviews your FAFSA application. Merit-based aid is usually provided in the form of scholarships.

    I.   *FAFSA*
           Free Application for Federal Student Aid, or FAFSA, is a form of aid that requires an application during the college admissions process.

II. *Scholarships*

These can be divided into two main categories: need-based scholarships and merit-based scholarships. Need-based scholarships are given out with consideration to your financial situation, but also take into account other things such as essays, grades, and awards. Merit-based scholarships on the other hand purely focus on your achievements. They don't take into consideration your family's income. Most people think of scholarships as something that you can only apply to when you are applying to college for the first time and that's just not true. You can continue to apply for school-sponsored or third-party scholarships even when you are enrolled in college.

III. *Grants*

A grant is a type of financial assistance that does not have to be paid back. The vast majority of grants come from the public sector.

Pell grants are the largest and most wide-reaching type of grant. Directed towards low-income college freshmen, these grants can provide up to $5,500 in benefits. Financially challenged students will often be awarded the Federal Supplemental Educational Opportunity Grant, in addition to Pell grants. These types of grants offer an extra annual benefit of $4,000.

IV. *Student Loans*

Student loans are taken out to obtain money in order to attend a certain university. You must repay the loan as well as the unpaid interest by a certain date. There are two different types of student loans: federal student loans and private student loans. Federal student loans are loans that are offered by the federal government, whereas private student loans are given by lenders like banks and credit unions. Generally, private student loans are much more costly than federal student loans.

There are various other college expenses that you will have to face. Do not forget to take into account daily expenditures, such as laundry and mobile phone bills, as well as school expenses such as books, supplies, and housing needs.

Furthermore, remember that you can always write a formal appeal letter and even make a phone call to your college to ask them to provide you with more financial aid, by emphasizing your financial situation and why you can make an impact on the school. There are also various other private scholarships that you may be able to obtain from businesses and nonprofit organizations. You can usually learn more about these with a simple search on the internet or by asking a guidance counselor.

SECTION 3:
INVESTMENT BASICS

Investment is a unique form of income as it is one where you can use your current wealth to grow even more wealth. One phrase you'll hear a lot in the financial world is "don't work for your money, make your money work for you". This is the basic principle of investment: the accumulation of wealth through the manipulation of pre-existing wealth.

Investment has many aspects to it, but the most prominent is risk. This is where investment draws heavy parallels with gambling. In investment, not a lot of information is certain, and no one can predict exactly what will happen in the future. While it may seem crazy that the world's richest are 'gambling' with their money, smart planning and using statistics, probability, and research can allow all of us to become the safest and smartest kind of gamblers. In this section, we will take a look at the relationship between risk and return, different vehicles of investment, and how to start investing.

Chapter 8
Risk vs. Return

There are many anecdotes and stories about people buying a previously obscure stock when it was worth only a few cents and making millions at its peak. While these stories might be true, they are almost as rare as winning the lottery and come with a lot more risk involved than just losing a few bucks on a scratch-off ticket. If there is one thing to know about the stock market, it's this: timing the market is impossible. Nobody can predict when the market is going to crash, or when it's going to continue to rally without losses for a month. With this being said, there are ways to get a good estimate of the market, which will allow you to control the risk you take on financially.

Your appetite for risk will determine your investing preferences. The basic concept behind risk and return is this: the higher your risk is, the higher your maximum yield or income returned can be, and conversely, the lower your risk is, the lower your returns will be. Does this mean you should settle for the measly 0.05% interest rate on your savings account, just so you don't risk losing some money? No. Although some low-risk investments like bonds and CD's (Certificate of Deposits) are guaranteed to give you some return, they often barely make up for currency inflation. We'll talk about the pros and cons of different approaches to investing in this section, as well as the power of compounding in investment.

It is key you make sure not to risk more than you can handle; it's especially important to make sure you can afford the potential losses that can result from such risky investments. Take famed investment YouTuber Matthew Jay for example. In efforts to display high returns to his fans, Jay continuously put money into high-risk ventures including things like biotechnology companies, niche technology startups, and obscure cryptocurrencies. As a result, due to multiple failures throughout his portfolio, the $150,000 he put in was reduced to a mere value of $50,000. This decimated his portfolio and acts as a forewarning to you and anyone else who may be thinking that these risky ventures are an easy way to make money.

Short-Term Strategies vs. Long-Term Strategies

A clear distinction between investment strategies is their time frame. Specifically, there are two kinds of strategies: short-term and long-term. These both have a fundamental relationship between their risk and return. Short-term strategies function to create returns as fast as possible. However, this comes with massive risk and such unstable strategies can only provide high returns for so long. On the other hand, there are less risky and more sustainable long-term investment strategies. This gets rid of risk and is more sustainable over time. It also has the added benefit of avoiding short-term capital gains tax which is only applicable to short-term investments. Additionally, through the principle of compounding, as we will discuss below, long-term strategy is more sustainable, less risky, and highly effective over time.

Power of Compounding

Time in the market beats timing the market. If you want high returns, but can't afford to lose a lot of money, all hope is not lost. It's just time to change your perception of investing. Rather than taking on risky high-return investments in a market that can be volatile or quick to change, it's better to just compound your investment in a safer environment. You may be wondering what we mean when we say compounding. This process is quite simple. Rather than taking the returns you make and pocketing them, you reinvest them back into your original investment. This creates a snowball effect where even if your return rate stays the same, you'll be getting more and more money back in the long run. This all comes without increasing risk. Picture this: you make a small snowball and push it down a snowy hill. It may start small, and slowly crawl down the hill, but little by little it starts getting bigger. It eventually gets bigger and bigger until the point that it's increasing by massive amounts, even if it's not growing at a faster rate. By continuing your snowball of investment, by compounding the investment you have rather than cashing it out, one day you may just end up with an avalanche of wealth.

Appreciation vs. Depreciation

Appreciation is when an asset's value increases over time, whereas depreciation is when an asset's value decreases over time. For example, appreciation occurs when there is a great demand for an asset, reduced supply of that asset, inflation, or changes in interest rates. Depreciation occurs basically as a result of the opposite of each. An example of a depreciating asset is a vehicle because it will usually lose most of its value over time. When someone makes money from selling an appreciated asset, it is referred to as a capital gain. On the other hand, capital loss occurs when someone sells an asset after it depreciates.

Chapter 9
Types of Securities

Securities are financial instruments that are bought and sold on a public exchange market. They are usually classified as either debt or equity instruments, in which you, as an investor, either provide a 'loan' or become a shareholder in the business.

Although in the past, trading securities has been mostly limited to the financially knowledgeable and wealthy upper class, nowadays, trading securities is one of the easiest ways to invest. A lot of the assets mentioned below are tradable through different types of brokerages.

Although the financial world has a lot of intricacies, we hope to educate you on what's necessary to understand as an investor. A lot of the information below on securities is simplified, but it includes the most crucial components.

Stocks

When people bring up the word 'investment', the stock market is one of the most common concepts that pop up. Although the reality of the stock market is incredibly complex, you only need to understand a few basic concepts of the stock market to start investing in it.

Also known as equity or shares, stocks represent ownership in an entity. When you buy a stock, you are essentially buying a piece of a company. In a very generalized sense, the value of a stock correlates with the value of a company. As a company expands and gains a higher book value, or the worth of its combined assets, its stock mirrors that same growth in its monetary value. That's the basic way people make money off of the stock market—by buying shares when the stock price is low and selling them when it grows.

Obviously, a company's growth can be overshadowed by an overall economic downturn. This is why it is also useful to understand the position of the stock market at a given time. A bull market is when prices are increasing, where typical investors buy low and sell high in order to generate revenue. On

Types of Securities

the other hand, a bear market is when prices are decreasing, and typical investors lose money.

It is important to note that not all companies are tradeable on the stock market. Companies must be a certain type of corporation in order to do so. Before these corporations can be publicly traded, they must hold an event called an Initial Public Offering (IPO), where they first allow outside investors to purchase their stock.

Another method of generating income through stocks is through dividends. Numerous companies pay their stockholders a small amount of money at set dates throughout the year; these payments are known as dividends. Dividends are given out to investors who have maintained possession of a stock through a certain date, and the total amount is calculated as a percentage of their holdings.

Companies use stocks as a means for raising funds. By selling ownership of a company, the money received can be used to pay off debt, create new services/products, or even grow their business into new markets.

Stocks can be a lot more volatile than other securities. However, certain established companies like Apple and Microsoft are incredibly reliable and have more stable growth than others; such companies are called blue-chip stocks. On the other hand, highly risky stocks that are valued at under five dollars per share are known as penny stocks.

Mutual Funds

One of the key concepts of investing is diversification. The cliche to not "put all your eggs in one basket" is applicable here. By investing all or a majority of your money into one company, you take the risk of bringing the value of your portfolio down, in the case where that one company does poorly in the market. By spreading your wealth into different assets, you lower the risk of your investment. This basic principle is manifested in a security called Mutual Funds.

A mutual fund is a form of investment that consists of pooling money into an externally managed portfolio of stocks. When you invest in a mutual fund, your capital is spread through the mutual fund's diversified portfolio which invests in different assets. The particular way in which an investment group chooses what types of investments to invest in is called asset allocation.

Let's take a look at a really basic example. Say you invested in a mutual fund that has their portfolio distributed like the following: 25% in Apple, 25% in Microsoft, and 50% in Tesla. If you were to invest $1000 into this mutual fund, it would be like purchasing $250 worth of Apple, $250 worth of Microsoft, and $500 worth of Tesla. Pretty easy, right?

One catch to mutual funds, however, is that they often have a fee attached to investing in them, typically ranging from 0%-2.5%. The advantage of mutual funds is that they are managed by expert financial analysts, so paying a small fee is usually worth it in the long run. You can figure out how expensive certain mutual funds are relative to their actual value by looking at the expense ratio. The expense ratio is the total cost of the mutual fund divided by the total value of the mutual fund. You want to look for funds with lower expense ratios that are still managed by qualified professionals.

Bonds

Bonds are the connections we share and cherish with our loved ones. Psych, this is a finance book, not a book about your feelings. Bonds are financial assets issued when the government or a corporation requests to borrow money. This is one of the most common examples of a debt-security, as an investor 'lends' money by purchasing the bond, with an agreement to receive regular interest payments as well as the face value of the bond by the time of expiration.

When a bond is first issued, it is given a maturity date at which the bond issuer must pay back the face value of the bond. The interest payments made to bondholders may be either fixed or variable and are determined by the bond's agreement. Bonds can either have short-term (<5 years), intermediate-term (5-10 years), or long-term (>10 years) 'expiration' periods.

Typically, the longer a bond's maturity period is, the higher the returns will be. The reason for this is that there is more risk associated with holding bonds for longer periods of time. Variable interest rates could severely decline over a decade, economic inflation could end up counteracting the interest payments gained over time, or the bond-issuer can even default on the bond, leaving you with a great loss of money. With that being said, this risk is generally a lot less than that associated with stocks, since the return is also a lot lower.

Exchange-Traded Funds

An Exchange-Traded Fund (ETF) is a security that monitors the performance of an underlying asset or group of assets. These can be traded on an exchange like stocks at the very same trading hours. The majority of ETFs fall into one of four categories: index, industry, regional, or commodity. Index ETFs monitor the performance of index funds such as the NASDAQ Composite or the Dow Jones Industrial Average. Industry ETFs track the averages of certain sectors like Biotechnology or the Information Technology industry. Regional ETFs typically track the benchmark index of a certain country or state. Finally, commodity ETFs allow you to invest in funds that track the value of physical commodities like gold or oil.

ETFs are similar to mutual funds in that they can monitor a wide pool of assets, as well as various types of securities, such as stocks and bonds. Your investment closely reflects the rise and fall of the various assets in your ETF, but not exactly. That's because when you acquire an ETF, you're not buying the assets it represents; instead, you're buying the fund itself.

Options

Options are an advanced type of security known as a derivative. They are directly tied to the value of an underlying asset, so their value is 'derived' from it. This security is a little bit more complicated than the previous ones, as it involves a contract between two parties, a buyer and a seller, and has a lot of moving parts. Although underlying assets in an option may be tied to securities like bonds or commodities, we'll be sticking with stock options for the sake of simplicity and practicality.

An individual option contract always represents what's known as a 'lot' of the underlying stock, which is a bundle of 100. Keep this in mind for now, as it will make sense for the explanations later.

Options contracts are typically one of two types: a call option or a put option. Once again, for simplicity and practicality, we'll look at these two types from the buyer's perspective. The buyer of a call option expects the stock to rise in value in the future. This option has what's called a strike price, a benchmark in the stock's price that has to be crossed in order for the option to be usable. Since the call option is in favor of the stock to rise, the strike price is always set higher than the current market rate of the stock. If the market rate of the stock passes the strike price, the option is now "In the Money" (ITM) and can be executed. If the contract is executed, the option buyer now buys one lot of the underlying asset at the strike price. This is an important development as the buyer can now make a profit if he sells his lot.

For a put option, the buyer expects the stock to go down in value. This time, for the stock to be ITM, it actually has to go below the strike price. This is because a put option grants the buyer the option to sell, rather than buy a lot of the underlying stock. Put options are typically used as insurance for downturns in the market since it grants the buyer the ability to sell at the strike price in case the stock falls far below it.

Now you might be wondering, if such powerful financial instruments can be used to invest and protect your wealth, what's the catch? Well, in order to buy options, you have to pay a small amount as a premium for each stock. This payment goes to the person originally writing the option (the person selling it to you) and can't be taken back. If the option never goes past the strike price or the contract expires before it is executed, then the buyer of the contract simply loses the money he put towards the premium.

Chapter 10
How to Invest

Now that you've learned about some of the basics behind financial investment, you probably can't wait to create your snowball of investment, but where should you start? You can't exactly just go call a company and ask to buy their stock.

While investment is a great way to set yourself up for the future, there are many moving parts within the investment machine including structures such as brokerages that act as 'stock stores'. Thus, you must understand the intricacies of this process to ensure you make the most of your money. In this chapter, we will be walking you through the way you invest, what you can invest in, and how to employ different strategies to get the returns you are seeking. In the future, if you feel as if you need more expertise, you can consult with a registered investment adviser who will provide investment and various financial services.

One important note, however, is that you can't open an investment account if you are still a minor. However, it is possible to get a parent or guardian to open one on behalf of you, where you can manage funds in the portfolio.

Brokerages

A brokerage is a firm or business that works between an investor and a stock exchange as a medium. Most of your transactions related to investing have to go through a brokerage in order to actually be processed. A brokerage account is a type of investment account that can be opened using a brokerage firm. The account holder may instruct a broker or firm to authorize trades.

An e-brokerage is a specific kind of brokerage that allows people to buy and sell stocks as well as gather investment information from its online website or app. There are different reasons people may prefer a traditional brokerage, but nowadays, most people invest through e-brokerages. Some of the most common ones are Robinhood, Fidelity, and TD Ameritrade.

Types of Orders

When dealing with securities such as stocks and ETFs that are listed on exchanges, you must place orders of when to buy or sell and based on what conditions. These orders can typically only execute during trading hours, but there are some exceptions to this. U.S. stock markets are typically open from 9:30 a.m. to 4:00 p.m. EST. However, certain trading platforms allow for trading during pre-market (usually from 8:00 a.m. to 9:30 a.m. EST) and after-hours (4:00 p.m. to 6:00 p.m. EST).

Orders that you place can have one of two time-frames: a day order or a Good-Till-Cancelled (GTC) order. Day orders are orders that expire after the regular trading day ends. GTC orders are orders that don't expire until they are canceled, however, most brokers have a 30-90 day period after which they expire, which is used to make sure that forgotten orders are not executed. The reason an order can expire is that it was either unable to be processed or the conditions for its execution were not fulfilled.

You can set different conditions on your orders in order to develop certain strategies or safety nets for your investing, and this is through utilizing the different types of orders. Different types of orders can help make your trading strategy easier so that you don't have to be constantly monitoring the market. We are going to specifically focus on stock orders, as they are the most commonly tradable and have more advanced functions. These orders behave differently based on whether you are buying or selling stock.

I. *Market Order*

This type of order is the most basic. For a buy, it purchases the stock at the current price that the market lists the stock as. For a sell, it sells stock at the market price.

II. *Limit Order*

This type of order allows you to specify the price level at which you would like to purchase a stock. For a buy, the order is executed if the market price falls below that level. For a sell, the order will be executed if the market price goes above that level.

III. *Stop-Loss Order*

This type of order helps you to halt your losses completely and is typically used as a safety net in case the stock plummets or soars. For a buy, the order is fulfilled when the price exceeds a certain threshold. This is so that you can avoid potential losses by purchasing it now before it reaches its height. For a sell, the order is executed when it falls below a certain threshold. This allows you to cut your losses and sell the stock at a loss.

IV. *Stop-Limit Order*

This type of order allows you to set two variables. The basic concept behind this order is that if it goes above or below a certain price, it generates a limit order. So, in essence, it's an order that creates another order. For a buy, if the price rises above a certain level, it triggers a limit buy to be created at a price below that level. For a sell, if the price goes below a certain level, it triggers a limit sell to be created above that price. Don't worry about this that much, since this a pretty advanced type of order.

What Defines a Good Investment?

A smart financial investment fits within your own financial goals and budget, leading to profitability. Good investments have high chances of success with low risks, or at least ways to overcome that risk. You may face obstacles along the way such as a market downturn, but your investment should be able to bounce back from a hit. The value of your investment should increase over time.

If you want a few general guidelines to picking good long-term investments, make sure that it is valued at an equitable price, has room to grow and increase value over time, and generates regular income.

Common Strategies

I. *Macro-Based Investment*

In this strategy, investors work based on large sectors of the economy and invest based on its trends. Rather than investing in individual companies in an industry, these investors put money into the entire sector. For example, if the cybersecurity industry is doing well, these individuals will disperse capital through the entire sector instead of an individual company like McAfee. This same trend of viewing investment from a macroscopic perspective applies to the entirety of the economy. If the entirety of a country's economy is doing well, this type of investor will invest in diversified securities like mutual funds that represent the country.

II. *Company-Level Investment*

This type of strategy is more applicable to advanced investments, where investors can recognize the intrinsic values of a company's success and thus, will invest in the company regardless of the macroeconomic view of the stock market.

III. *Fundamental Investment*

This investment method is where investors view stocks as more than just their market value. Specifically, this happens in two ways. First, based on the financial statements of the company. This allows investors to see the real value of the stock and swoop in if the market value is higher. Second, based on investors' speculation. This is when fundamental investors view market speculation critically. When bad news breaks out in certain investment sectors, investors often jump out very quickly, but fundamental investors are not so easily spooked. When market panic causes the value of the stock to dip below its intrinsic value, they swoop in again because they think the intrinsic value of the stock determines its worth rather than its market value.

IV. *Contrarian Investment*

This is one of those high-risk, high-reward strategies that would in most cases be better to avoid. A contrarian investor invests in sectors of the economy that most people are betting against. While this lets them pick up assets when they are undervalued, there is a good chance that they will devalue. However, on the off chance that one of these sectors gets reinvigorated, these investors get massive returns.

V. *Dividend Investment*

Buying stocks that pay out dividends or ones that pay out their profits to stockholders is a perfect investment strategy if you are looking to make continuous, stable returns. Regardless of the stock value, you still get money back based on your equity allowing you to circumvent stock market volatility if the company is doing well. However, beware that many investors think that strong stocks with high dividends are overvalued, but depending on the scenario, that may just be the case for your prospective investments.

VI. *Index Investment*

There is not much to this, but we did want to include it since it is one of the most commonly used investment strategies. Through index investment, you simply just invest in various index funds and let your money do the work for you.

Advanced Strategies

These strategies require huge sums of money, amounts that you will likely not be close to having as a teenager, but we wanted to discuss them so you can gain familiarity with them in the future.

I. *Savior Plan Investment*

This is when a party invests huge sums of money into a company that is about to fail or default. While this may sound counterintuitive, if an investing party becomes the majority shareholder, it can reorganize the company to attempt to make it profitable. While this has risks, through overhauling a company through a savior plan, investors can make tremendous profits. An example of this is when Warren Buffet took over Wells Fargo when it was financially floundering during the 2008 recession.

II. *Arbitrage*

An arbitrager is a person who profits from the differences in conversion rates between two currencies. To illustrate this, let's use a simplified analogy: the dollar and the rupee. Let's go ahead and assume that purchasing one rupee costs a dollar but converting back gives us two dollars. Again, this is grossly oversimplified and exaggerated for the sake of clarity but doing this conversion over and over again will turn the small discrepancy into massive returns.

III. *Quantitative, Statistical and Machine Learning Methods*

Machine learning and statistical methods are types of analytical techniques that let you sort through massive amounts of data with the help of machines and algorithms. Analysts in this field, typically large investment firms, can use this data to predict market trends and adapt investment strategies to what big data predicts will be successful.

Chapter 11
Reading Financial Statements

In this chapter, we will be discussing how to read financial statements. These statements are published documents of a business' corporate activity and business ventures and are usually utilized by firms and agencies for help with tax and financing purposes. There are 4 main types of financial statements, which we will be going over in detail.

What are Financial Statements?
Financial statements are a compilation of summarized reports regarding the financial performance, financial situation, and cash flow of an entity. These statements are used primarily to assess a company's ability to generate revenue and whether the company can pay back its debts, if necessary. Also, the specifics of commercial transactions are included in these statements. Specifically, the standard set of financial statements include balance sheets, income statements, statements of cash flows, and statements of change in equity.

Importance
Financial reviewers use this financial data to make projections of a company's future stock price. These statements are primarily utilized by analysts and investors to measure an organization's financial stability.

Balance Sheet
The balance sheet is one of the most basic financial statements that give you an overview of the business. First, let's start by defining some key terms. An asset is any kind of property or possession that has value and is owned by the individual or entity filing it as such. Liabilities are the money that a company or individual must pay to outside parties. The equation used to calculate the total value of assets is *Assets = Liabilities + Equity*. This might seem counterintuitive, but you should realize that this equation does not mean that your assets

are the same things as your liabilities and equity, but rather the worth of your assets is equal to the value of your liabilities and equity.

```
                          TEDDY FAB INC.
                          BALANCE SHEET
                         December 31, 2100

    ASSETS                              LIABILITIES AND SHAREHOLDERS' EQUITY
    Current assets                      Current liabilities
      Cash and cash equivalents  $ 100,000   Accounts payable           $ 30,000
      Accounts receivable          20,000    Notes payable                10,000
[1]   Inventory                    15,000    Accrued expenses              5,000   [3]
      Prepaid expense               4,000    Deferred revenue              2,000
      Investments                  10,000    Total current liabilities    47,000
      Total current assets        149,000
                                            Long-term debt              200,000
    Property and equipment
      Land                         24,300   Total liabilities           247,000
      Buildings and improvements  250,000
      Equipment                    50,000   Shareholders' Equity
[2]   Less accumulated depreciation (5,000)   Common stock                10,000
                                              Additional paid-in capital  20,000   [4]
    Other assets                              Retained earnings          197,100
      Intangible assets             4,000     Treasury stock              (2,000)
      Less accumulated amortization  (200)
                                            Total liabilities and shareholders' equity  $ 472,100  [5]
    Total assets                $ 472,100
```

1. The first section lists some common assets including cash, market securities or short-term stocks that can be liquidated quickly, inventory or sellable items in the company's custody, and finally accounts receivable or legally enforceable payments the company should receive from other entities. This adds up to total current assets or assets which can be liquidated within a year.
2. This part of the balance sheet covers smaller assets in this case property such as a company's building. There are other assets not listed which still benefit the company, but do not fit into any of the previous categories. These smaller assets in addition to total current assets results in total assets.
3. The third segment of the document begins to cover losses to the company in terms of liability and stockholder sharing. In the first part of these sheet current liabilities or liabilities that need to be paid back within 12 months. These include accounts payable or payments the company legally must make to other entities, accrued expenses or expenses that have not paid during a previous accounting period, and finally unearned revenue or money owed to the company from a customer

who received their services or product, but has not paid. In total these three items equal total current liabilities.
4. This part covers two kinds of stocks being distributed by the company: treasury stock, which have been bought back by the company, and common stocks, which grant voting rights to stockholders within a company give equity to stockholders. Additionally, there are retained earnings which are profits leftover after dividends are paid to shareholders. Additional paid in capital represents the par value of the company's stock paid by an investor.
5. At the end of the balance sheet, all these added together result in the total liabilities and shareholder equity at the bottom of the sheet, which is the same value as the total assets.

Income Statement

Also referred to as a Profit and Loss (P&L) Statement, an income statement includes revenue, expenses, and loss transactions for a set time period. Specifically, an income statement includes various components: revenue, expenses, costs of goods, profit, and income. Sometimes, depreciation and earnings are also included. Below is an example of a P&L statement.

Metropolitan Arts and Crafts
Income Statement
For the Twelve Month Period Ending December 31, 20XX

[1]
Gross Sales	10,000	
less Sales Returns	500	
Net Sales		9,500

Cost of Goods Sold
Beginning Inventory	3,000	

[2]
Purchases	500	
Freight-In	300	
Storage	100	

Goods Available for Sale	3,900	
Less Ending Inventory	1,000	
Cost of Goods Sold		2,900
Gross Profit		6,600

General & Administrative Expenses:

[3]
Rent	500	
Wages	1,000	
Utilities	250	

Total General & Administrative Expenses		1,750
Total Expenses		4,650

[4] Net Income — 4,850

1. This first quarter of the statement represents the cash flowing into the business. Gross sales represents the total value of goods sold; on the other hand, the sales returns refers to the value of goods returned back to the seller. Net sales is calculated by subtracting the sales returns from the gross sales and displays the total flow of cash out of the selling entity.
2. This part of the income statement includes all of the costs involved in creating the business's product/service. The beginning inventory represents the current value of the goods that are presently held. Below that, all other costs associated with creating new goods are listed. All of these separate costs added together make up the Cost of Goods Sold (COGS). Lastly, gross profit is calculated by subtracting COGS from the net sales in section 1.
3. The third segment of the statement displays general and administrative costs in this case being rent, wages, and utilities (costs associated with operating a business).
4. The fourth part of the income statement includes the total expenses, which encompasses every expense the business accrues. The last line indicates the net income, which is equal to the total expenses subtracted from the gross profit.

Statement of Cash Flow

This type of statement includes all of the outgoing expenses and incoming capital that a company generates and tracks the amount of capital within a business. All expenses and gains from these statements come under operations (such as taxes), investments (such as business equipment), or lastly from financing (such as dividends). Cumulatively, this lets businesses track changes in capital and net capital circulating within the business.

Below is an example cash flow statement.
First on this sheet we see the amount of capital generated from income or the money the company got for its service or product minus the expenses (this can be adapted to a person's income as well, but it commonly is not). Depreciation expense is the funding removed during the accounting process.

Bob's Donut Shoppe, Inc.
Cashflow Statement
As of the 31st January 2020

		$	$
1	Net Income	(6,050)	
	Add back: depreciation expense	500	
			(5,550)
2	**Changes in working capital**		
	Increase in accounts receivable	(3,000)	
	Increase in prepaid rent	(750)	
	Increase in inventory	(18,800)	
	Increase in accounts payable	19,000	
	Increase in accrued expenses	700	
	Increase in unearned income	9,000	
	Net changes in working capital		6,150
3	**Total Cash from Operations**		600
	Investing Cashflow		
4	Renovations and improvements	(25,000)	
	Cash from investing		**(25,000)**
	Financing Cashflow		
	Issuance of common stock	50,000	
5	Issuance of long-term liability	24,500	
	Dividends paid	(500)	
	Cash from investing		**74,000**
	Net Increase / decrease in cash flow		49,600
6	Opening cash		-
	Closing cash		**49,600**

Reading Financial Statements

1. Here is listed the net income amount. Below that is noted an add back expense of depreciation that covers funding that is added to the asset's value.
2. In the second segment of the cash flow statement, changes in working capital or difference in money available for operations from one accounting period to the next are recorded. It lists the increase in accounts receivable, the increase in prepaid rent, the increase in inventory, the increase in accounts payable, the increase in accrued expenses, and the increase in unearned revenue. The sum of these factors results in the net changes in working capital.
3. The third part indicates the total cash from operations, which is the difference between working capital and net income as seen above.
4. The fourth segment includes the investing cashflow, which refers to capital directed to improving internal business processes and efficiency.
5. The fifth part of the cash flow statement displays the financing cashflow. This accounts for stocks being bought and sold, liabilities issued on these stocks, as well as dividends paid from them.
6. The last segment includes the net increase/decrease and the opening cash. Below that, the closing cash is listed, which indicates the total current cash a business has during the marking period.

Statement of Changes in Equity

The statement of changes in equity is a list of a company's beginning and ending equity balances recorded over a period. Furthermore, over a certain duration, this statement maintains a record of other relevant revenue and the effects of changes in accounting strategies found during that period.

Annual Report

An annual report is a detailed summary of the accomplishments and financial reports of a company from the previous year. It is generated on an annual basis and is made available to shareholders and stakeholders. Annual reports are also used as tools to show shareholders, investors, or donors and to display their brand to staff, consumers, and others as public resources for companies.

SECTION 4:
CAREER-ORIENTED FINANCE

Becoming an adult has lots of responsibilities, but you already know that, so we are going to talk about responsibilities specific to career finance in this section. Specifically, we will be addressing finance related to your income, assets, and taxes.

Since you're likely a minor, the chances are your parents cover most of this stuff for you. You've probably never had to directly concern yourself with providing for other people, making sure your property is managed properly, or even working a full-time job. However, as soon as you turn 18, a lot of this *will* involve you, and we want you to be prepared.

Many students complain about how most public education prepares them for the wrong stuff. Shouldn't understanding how to file your taxes come before learning how to differentiate logarithmic functions? Yes. Yes, it should. So, prepare to be educated.

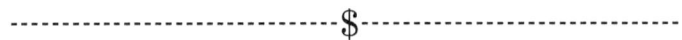

Chapter 12
Getting a Job

Although there are various important aspects of finding the right job for you, knowing how to effectively search for a job is extremely important. You should look for a job that aligns with your qualifications, but also meets your needs. This chapter will help you learn more about the different job search methods and application techniques.

Rather than trying to fill out hundreds of applications hoping to get hired by one employer, you should start by taking the time to determine exactly what position would fit you the best. If you select a field that you enjoy working on, you will have a much easier time with online searching.

Building a Resume

When creating a resume, you should choose between creating a chronological or functional resume. A chronological resume is a traditional resume that includes your experiences organized by date. On the other hand, a functional resume organizes your experiences by skill. Most people choose to use a chronological resume, but if you lack work experience, you may want to use a functional resume.

We've broken down the process of resume-building into a simple 4-part system.

1. *Main Header*

This should consist of your name, phone number, email address, and home address. You can also include extra information like a URL to your LinkedIn profile.

2. *Resume Objective*

This should be used to explain why you are looking for the applied role and specific goals you hope to accomplish through your future occupation. For younger individuals such as yourself, you may want to talk about future professional aspirations and how this kind of opportunity can help you get there.

3. *Work Experience & Skills*
Include a list of all of your work experiences, previous education, and skills. You should only write ones related to your career or ones that display qualities designated for the job. Additionally, make sure you quantify your impact on your previous occupations to let your hiring manager gauge your ability objectively.

4. *Awards and Certifications*
Lastly, include any significant awards or certifications that you have been given. Make sure to include the award's title, level of recognition, and date. Additionally, briefly explain the impact of the award to the reader.

Here is an example of a professional resume.

Nils Clasen

- **Phone number:** 555-555-5555
- **Email address:** hello@kickresume.com

Profile

Performance-driven and dedicated entrepreneur with a proven track record of success in developing and leading a successful technology startup, experienced in all aspects of business management. Possess a strong attention to detail and accuracy, exceptional analytical and critical-thinking skills, and the important ability to work and perform well under pressure and in fast-paced environments.

Work experience

10/2016 - present
Berlin, Germany

Founder & CEO
Clasen Technologies, Inc.
- Founded a company which specializes in the development of software applications that use machine learning and artificial intelligence to help different organizations to automate their processes and operations.
- Managing and coordinating all aspects of a business, including marketing, finance, and strategy development.
- Creating annual business plans, hiring and training new personnel, and representing the company at various industry events and conferences.
- Identifying and communicating with potential clients and business partners and performing any other necessary duties.
- Clients include Netflix, IBM, Samsung, BMW, Audi, etc.

Education

09/2015 - 05/2017
Berlin, Germany

High School
Gustav-Freytag-Oberschule
Dropped out to pursue entrepreneurship
Clubs and Societies: Business Club, Debate Society, Fitness Club

Skills

LANGUAGES
- German — Native
- English — Full
- Spanish — Elementary

INTERPERSONAL SKILLS
- Ability to Work under Pressure
- Communication Skills
- Critical Thinking
- Leadership Skills
- Problem-solving
- Teamwork
- Time Management

PROGRAMMING LANGUAGES
- C++, PHP
- Java, JavaScript
- Python, Swift

Writing a Cover Letter

A cover letter is an additional document that is usually submitted along with your resume when you apply for a job. This document highlights your main qualifications and explains why you are fit for the role . You should create a unique cover letter for each job you apply for as you want to cater to a specific employer's requirements. Below are the specific details that should be included in a persuasive cover letter.

1. Header with your contact information: name, address, phone, and email
2. Salutation to greet your employer
3. Opening paragraph introducing yourself and the job title that you are applying for
4. Explanation for how you learned about the job and why you feel you are a good fit for the position
5. Proposition of what you can offer to the employer and why you believe you should be chosen; be sure to include hard numbers from your previous experiences (ex. I increased direct to-consumer sales by 30%) to give your potential employer an exact scope of your qualifications
6. Thank the employer for considering you for the position and end your letter with your handwritten signature and typed name

Finding Opportunities

Finding a job may seem like a daunting task, but with the correct strategies, it is very achievable. If you're searching for work, the internet is an excellent place to begin. You can list your credentials and qualifications on online sites like Indeed, Monster, and Glassdoor to find a suggested match from prospective employers. Some of these websites also allow users to filter job listings based on factors such as expected starting salary, job level (part-time or full-time), and employment location. However, despite the digitization of the job market, even old-school methods such as looking through a newspaper or asking acquaintances can help you find a job opening you may be interested in.

How to Interview

The most critical part of a job application is the interview process. It serves as a final check prior to employment. Before your interview, make sure you've done your homework on both the business and the position. Answering questions in a succinct, honest, and informative manner is crucial, so spend some time studying common interview questions so you can prepare your responses. Try to practice or roleplay an interview with someone beforehand so that you are well prepared. After the interview, you will likely be asked if you have any questions for the interviewee. While it is great if you have questions that came to you during the interview, make sure you have some pre-prepared backups so that you can demonstrate interest to your interviewer.

References

Almost every single job you apply to will ask for outside references to verify your qualifications with a third party. Thus, you must build quality relationships with people like your professors and prior employers. You must build trust with those individuals so that they are willing to help you pursue future opportunities.

Employee Mindset

Essentially, getting a job is a marketing process. You must be able to entice your potential employer and consider the hiring process from their point of view. You must demonstrate your merit and skills to someone unfamiliar with you. It is up to you to promote yourself in the manner you want, and for the most part only when doing that properly, can you land a job. However, just because you got an offer, doesn't mean you can let go and 'chill'—that's when the real work starts. Ensure that you are cooperative and inspired from the moment you receive an offer.

How to Deal With Rejection

At first, don't be startled if you get rejected from a job. It's not because you didn't try hard enough or weren't competent enough, rather it's simply that most employers value experience over any other factors. For many people, it takes dozens of applications to land a job, so don't be discouraged. Just pick yourself up, no matter the situation, and keep applying. Even if you have a slim chance of getting a job, apply for it with a positive mindset.

Chapter 13
Taxes

One of the most dreaded aspects of reaching adulthood is having to file your annual taxes, and we're not going to lie to you, it's not a fun experience. Though, however tedious the process is, it can be made easier and less time-consuming if you know what you're doing.

Tax has existed in societies since before paper money was invented, and for good reasons. Taxes may be used to pool a community's resources and assets, allowing communities to build public facilities and shared spaces. In today's financial world, almost any financial decision you make will be influenced by tax considerations. We'll go through what taxes are in this chapter, as well as the differences between different types of taxes and how you'll deal with them in the future.

What are Taxes?

Taxes are a certain percentage of money taken from monetary transactions involving certain goods, services, incomes, properties, or sales, used by the government. The government uses these funds for building public infrastructure, education, the military, and social welfare.

Taxes are classified into three categories depending on which level of government collects them: local, state, or federal. These taxes are used for a myriad of purposes.

At the federal level, social security, public health care, and national defense are the main areas where taxes are allocated. States receive some funds from the federal government, but they also have the option of taxing their citizens directly to finance education, transportation, and other aspects of state government. Finally, municipalities use tax revenue to fund the construction of local highways, the operation of public schools, and the management of police and fire departments.

In America, individual income tax, sales tax, property tax, and corporate income tax are the four most prevalent taxes.

For the sake of simplicity, we will be mainly explaining the first three, as it deals with how you, as an individual, will be taxed, but we have summarized some of the other types as well.

What is the IRS?

It's a well-known fact that there are two things you can't avoid: death and the IRS. The IRS, or Internal Revenue Service, is a federal agency that specializes in tax collection and tax enforcement. These organizations frequently perform duties such as tax audits, cooperate with other agencies, and report to track down tax fraud and process tax inflow. There is a lot of fear around the IRS as it is often represented as some sort of boogeyman that will come for you if you fail to file your taxes, but this just isn't true.

While the IRS is responsible for enforcing the law, it also provides a great deal of assistance and grace to those who are in need. On their website, they have a number of tools related to tax filing that can help you understand the procedure, and they also grant exceptions to people in difficult situations.

Progressive and Proportional Taxes

Progressive taxes are taxes where the rate increases as the primary taxable amount increases. We see progressive taxes in real life in the form of federal income tax. The federal income tax uses a bracket system, where people whose income falls within a certain range have to pay a certain percentage of tax. As this range gets higher, the percentage also increases.

Unlike progressive taxes, proportional taxes are taxes where the rate stays the same no matter the taxable amount. Sales tax typically uses the proportional system. In the city of Dallas, for example, whether you buy a chocolate bar for $1, or buy a 4K television for $1000, you pay the same percentage of sales tax (8.25%).

It's important to realize that when dealing with proportional and progressive tax rates, we are talking about a percentage, and not a dollar amount; this means there is never a flat rate for taxes, say $1,000, but rather a proportion of your income.

Taxes

Below is an example of a progressive tax chart.

Taxable Income	Percentage Tax on Income
$0 - $9,950	10%
$9,951 - $40,525	12%
$40,526 - $86,375	22%
$86,376 - $164,925	24%
$164,926 - $209,425	32%
$209,426 - $523,600	35%
$523,601	37%

Personal Income Tax

These are taxes placed on an individual's earnings. This may come from sources including an individual's salary, the sale of an investment, or dividends from ownership of stocks. This is one of the national government's primary sources of revenue.

Income tax is a tax that is withheld from your paycheck monthly, based on what you claimed as your taxable income (which is done through your W-4). Income taxes are calculated at the end of a full calendar year (January-December) but are only filed on April 15. The reason for filing your income tax is to verify that the amount withheld from your income, matches the amount that you owe the government. If the amount paid is greater than what you owe, you are eligible for a tax refund, where the government gives you back the extra money. If the amount paid is less than what you owe, you will have to pay the IRS back the outstanding amount.

Payroll Tax

Mandated by the Federal Insurance Contributions Act (FICA), payroll taxes are taxes that are collected by one's employer. The tax can be divided into two categories: one for social security and another for Medicare. FICA is paid by both workers and employers, but only the employer is required to register it. Every month, a portion of the employee's salary is deducted, which is matched by the employer. This percentage changes annually and goes towards funding for social security

(6.2% contribution in 2019) and government-sponsored healthcare (1.45% contribution in 2019).

Below is an example of a pay stub, which includes tax deductions.

```
SMITH AND COMPANY, INC.
123 West Street Smalltown, CA  98765

EMPLOYEE          SOCIAL SECURITY NO.    PAY RATE              PAY PERIOD
Johnson, Bob  1   XXX-XX-6789            18.00  regular        1/7/XX to 1/13/XX
                                         27.00  overtime

EARNINGS   HOURS   AMOUNT                DEDUCTIONS            AMOUNT
Regular    40.00   720.00   2             Federal W/H           60.45
Overtime    2.00    54.00                 FICA                  47.99
                                      3   Medicare              11.22
GROSS EARNINGS:    774.00                 CA State W/H          10.04
TOTAL DEDUCTED:    213.29                 CA State DI            6.19
NET EARNINGS:      560.71                 401k                  77.40

SICK LEAVE:              4
24.00 HOURS AVAILABLE
```

1. At the top of the pay stub, identifying information about the employee and basic information surrounding their work information is printed. This allows for tracking in the payment system and also allows identification of specific employee circumstances.
2. Below we can see the employee's base earnings dependent on their pay rates.
3. The deductions here are referring to the sums of money going towards 401(k), state taxes, and payroll taxes. These are taken as percentages from the employee's earnings.
4. At the bottom left, we can see that a pay stub finishes off with the net earnings the employee is taking home after deductions are taken from the gross earnings. As you can also see, some sheets include sick days.

Capital Gains Tax

We briefly talked about capital gains tax in Section 2, but we'll take a deeper dive into the complexities here. Just like working a salaried job, investing is also an income-producing process, and therefore a taxable process. In fact, money made from investments is still considered a part of your personal income but taxed at a different rate than your traditional income. But before we get further in, let's concretely define this type of tax. Capital gains tax is a tax placed on money earned from the selling of an asset that has increased in value since its original purchase. These assets may include stocks, bonds, and even real estate properties.

There are two different kinds of capital gains: short-term and long-term. short-term capital gains occur after selling assets owned for less than a single year. These capital gains are taxed at the same rate as your regular income. On the other hand, long-term capital gains occur after selling assets owned for more than a single calendar year. These capital gains are usually taxed at a rate significantly lower than short-term gains but are still related to what income bracket you are in.

Property Tax

This type of tax is placed on real estate properties by state or municipal governments and is calculated according to the value of the property that is owned. Since real estate often has a large value tied to it, these taxes can come out to large sums that are due at the end of the year. However, the use of certain financial tools can reduce large property tax payments into smaller installments.

One such tool is an escrow account. Many mortgage lenders require you to either have one or open one with their institution, so that you can pay property taxes cumulatively, instead of being blindsided with a large payment at the end of the year. By paying 1/12th of your annual property tax to your escrow account monthly, you are giving the financial institution running your account enough money to cover that tax when it is due.

Sales Tax

This is a government-imposed tax on retail goods and services, which is collected by the retailer as the consumer makes a purchase. This amount is then provided to the state, on a monthly or quarterly basis. While certain states with high costs of living, like California and New York, have upwards of a

8% average sales tax, states like Alaska, Delaware, New Hampshire, Montana, and Oregon do not collect sales tax.

Other Taxes

I. *Corporate Tax*
    A corporate tax is a tax on a company's income. The taxes are placed on the net income of a corporation, which is calculated considering the cost of goods sold, general and administration expenditures, research and development expenses, depreciation, and operating costs.

II. *Tariff*
    A tariff is tax levied on imported goods at the national level. The federal government imposes these to counteract trade deficits or when a country imports more than it exports with foreign countries. For example, starting in 2017, the Trump administration placed tariffs on imported Chinese goods.

III. *Estate Tax*
    An estate tax is a tax on someone's property and assets taken after they pass away. This tax is collected for the transfer of the estate. These taxes are rather uncommon as they only apply to extremely expensive assets (> $12,000,000 in 2018) and also involve relatively high tax percentages, ranging from 20% to 40%.

Tax Breaks

The U.S. government and many other governments around the world often use certain incentives as a way to encourage certain financial behaviors or actions. One such incentive is a tax break. Tax breaks are deductions in the amount of taxes you have to pay and are given to individuals if they meet certain criteria.

Although taxes go towards the funding for many publicly shared facilities and programs, the government is still taking a cut out of your hard-earned money. If you want to earn more and keep more of your earnings, you should take any chance you can get to reduce the amount of taxes you pay. Although a controversial topic, the debate over whether the 'rich' should be taxed more is important to bring up here. Oftentimes, even with increased percentages, many wealthy people pay relatively low percentages of their actual income as taxes. The main method is through using tax breaks.

There are three types of tax breaks: a tax deduction, a tax exemption, and a tax credit.
- A tax deduction lowers the amount of gross income that may be taxable.
- A tax exemption protects a certain percentage of your revenue from being taxed.
- A tax credit directly takes away from the amount of tax you owe.

These three incentives can be given for a variety of different things in the United States, but they all must be applied for when filing your taxes.

How to File Your Taxes

Filing your taxes can be very confusing and even stressful, but there are many tax preparation services and online tax-filing platforms that can reduce the hassle of the process.

If you would like to file your taxes through a professional, hiring a Certified Public Accountant, or CPA is probably the best way to go. Going through a CPA is especially important if you are inexperienced with tax filing, as working on your own could lead to you committing accidental tax fraud.

There are also certain online platforms, such as Intuit and TurboTax, that can assist you while filing your taxes. However, you need to be a bit more careful and knowledgeable if you choose to follow this path. Online tax-filing platforms have many limitations and could lead to mistakes if you aren't being vigilant.

No matter what method you use to file your taxes, there are a couple of basic steps that you need to take. You will need to first obtain a W-2 form from your employer. This form is already filled out by your employer and contains information about your salary and the taxes withheld from your pay from that year. If you have any additional income, like from investments that you have sold, financial statements from those are also necessary. Finally, you should also collect any evidence related to taxes you want to write off.

Common Federal Tax Forms

I. *W-2*

This form is completed by your employer and displays the amount of tax deducted from your paycheck per year. You will need to request a W-2 from your employer when filing.

II. *W-4*

This form is used by employees to request their employer to deduct a specific, suitable amount of federal income tax from their composite check. This was referred to earlier as the withheld amount for income tax.

III. *W-9*

Unlike a W-4, W-9 forms are used by people who don't receive a regular salary, and work on a different payment structure. Freelance workers are an example of this.

IV. *1098*

This form lists the mortgage interest you paid to your lender over the year. It can also include student loan amounts and will help when determining the tax deductions you can make.

V. *1099*

This type of form is documentation of payments made from an entity, other than your employer, to yourself. This must be copied and sent out to the receiver and the Internal Revenue Service (IRS). This form is specifically used to document payments made for various sources of income including rental and sales payments.

Tax Audits

A tax audit is an analysis completed by the IRS of your filed tax return to verify your income and deduction amounts.

This occurs when the IRS chooses to look closely at your tax return.

Primarily, there are three specific types of audits: mail, office, and field. Mail audits are sent to individuals who make common mistakes when filing their taxes; 7/10 audits fall into this category. Office and Field audits are much more intrusive and usually involve the IRS looking through financial records to verify proper tax procedures were undertaken. The main contrast between these is that office audits are done at an IRS office while field audits are done at the homes and businesses of the 'auditees'.

Chapter 14
Buying a House

Buying a house is a financial milestone that will mark the beginning of your long-term asset portfolio. It is critical to make the right decision in this area as it very well could be the biggest financial decision you will have made so far. In this chapter, we will cover the basics of buying a house and walk you through the lesser-known but equally important financial responsibilities that accompany it.

Can You Afford Your Future Investment?
We are sorry to be the bearers of bad news, but you likely won't be able to purchase a house by yourself fresh out of college, as it takes time to build up savings and credit. There are many expenses associated with home buying, so you have to reach a certain financial threshold to even start considering it.

When buying a house, there are two major types of expenses: the first of which are the initial costs, including down payment and closing costs. Here are the specifics of each expense: a down payment is a type of payment that is made in the early stages of a large purchase. For a home, your down payment will be a certain amount requirement that will depend upon the type of mortgage and lender chosen. These loans can start from as little as 3%, but even this amount can be pretty large. Closing costs are paid to complete your mortgage, usually anywhere from 2% to 6%. Sometimes, you can ask the seller to pay all or some of your closing costs, which can be a big relief. Move-in costs should be allocated for miscellaneous expenses after moving in including purchasing furniture and upgrades.

After doing this, look at your current assets and determine an appropriate amount of money that you can spend on a house. There are many online calculators that you can use to help decide on a price range for your potential house after looking at your income, debt, down payment, and home specifications.

After handling initial costs, move on to see if you could afford the long-term costs of the house: the mortgage. Look at your current credit score to see if you can qualify for a certain mortgage and attain a friendly interest rate. After doing so, take a look at the various types of mortgages available. The main types include conventional mortgages which are suited for first-time homebuyers (usually 3% down), Federal Housing Administration loans which are used for small down payments (4%), and U.S. Department of Agriculture loans which are meant to be used for rural buyers. These loans can be set for different periods as we will discuss down below.

Mortgage Loans
We briefly mentioned how mortgage loans, or mortgages, function in Chapter 8, but there are more nuances to it that we'd like to bring up here. As a quick recap, a mortgage is a loan taken out in order to finance the purchase of a home. It typically has either a 15-year or 30-year term over which the loan is paid off. Within a mortgage, payments stay the same and are paid monthly, covering both interest and the principal.

Since mortgage payments are paid over a longer time period than regular loans, and monthly payments are equal, a special type of calculation called amortization is used. Amortization shows how your monthly mortgage payments are distributed between your principal and interest. At the beginning of your mortgage time period, most of your payments will go towards the interest, but as time passes, a larger portion of each payment will go towards the principal of the house.

Here is an example of a graph representing the distribution of payments between principal and interest.

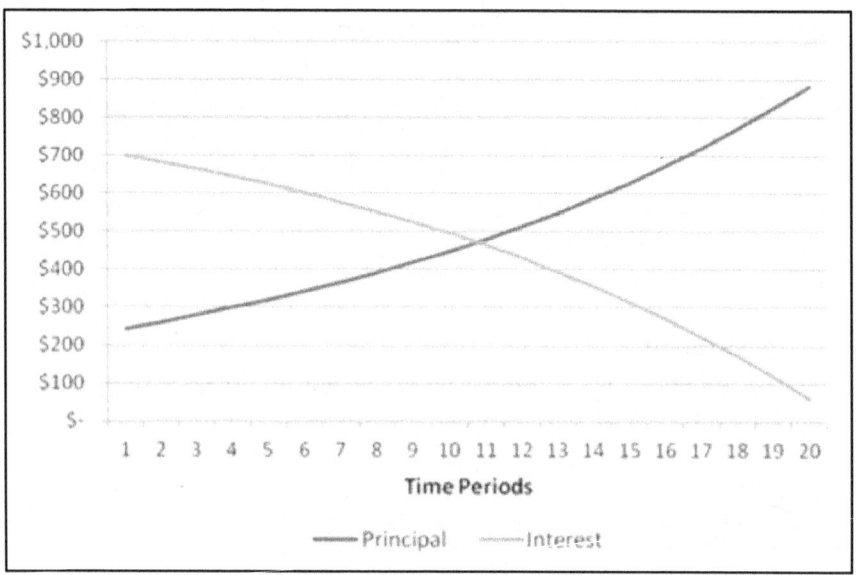

Another aspect of mortgages is the ability to replace your existing mortgage with a new one, a process known as refinancing. Refinancing a home allows for you to enter a new mortgage, typically with the hopes of reducing either your interest rate or payment period. While this can have many benefits, make sure to consider whether or not refinancing is a good idea for your personal situation.

First off, refinancing costs money. Mortgage payers require somewhere between 3%-6% of the loan principal as an initial payment, and there might even be other fees that accompany this. Additionally, if you are receiving a lower interest rate, your monthly payment will probably also decrease, but this might 'reset' your mortgage term as well. This means that you will have to essentially have to continue paying for another thirty or fifteen years. Another implication this has is that all the interest that went towards your original mortgage is lost. Since your monthly payments were amortized, the majority of your payments likely went towards interest.

Choosing a Real Estate Agent

Getting a real estate agent can make buying a house much easier, but it does come at a cost (literally). Real estate agents help mediate the process of homebuying between the buyer and seller, in order to ensure that all parties' needs are met. You will want to find an affordable agent, who has your best interests and budget in mind and will actively help you find a house best suited for you.

One of the ways you can do this is by reading online reviews. With reviews, you can verify the credibility of the individual or agency through the past experiences of other new or experienced homebuyers. Another great place to start is simply asking the homeowners around your current area or even the homeowners in the area you hope to move into. This will allow you to perspective and allow you to make the best decision possible.

New Home Trinity Relationship

In the real estate industry, when it comes to buying a newly built house, there are three main 'actors' interacting with each other and the house: the home builder, the real estate agent, and the home buyer. The builder is the party that deals with the actual construction and specifications of the new home. There are ways in which a homebuilder can go directly to the home buyer to sell a house, but most times, a real estate agent will act as a 'middleman' between the two parties. Real estate agents receive a commission from both the builder and the buyer (usually ranging between 5% to 6%), which is why it reduces costs when you eliminate the agent from the picture. Though ultimately you, the homebuyer, are the most important part of this triangular relationship. Whether or not you decide to buy a house is completely based on your thoughts and knowledge, which is why you should take your time when buying a home and not settle for mediocrity.

Choosing a Neighborhood

It's important to be realistic about how large of a purchase you can make when selecting a house. A rule of thumb is to spend a maximum of 28% of your monthly income on the monthly payment of your mortgage. Using this individual information, you can narrow down neighborhoods based on your price range using online platforms, your realtor, or even word of mouth.

If you feel that there are multiple areas with similar price ranges that you are satisfied with, make sure to analyze things like lifestyle, demographics, schools, and other factors to see if it is the right fit for you and your family.

Negotiating

There are many things that you can do to lower the cost of your home. While placing an offer, you can ask for advice from your realtor on a suitable amount under the list price. Additionally, during the inspection process, you can ask the seller to cover any repairs that are presented. When closing on your home, closing costs can be asked to be paid partially or in full. You should try to take advantage of the market if your chosen home has a small number of buyers interested or if the market is down. Keep in mind that each realtor, for used home sales, will receive a commission of 2%-3%, which may be a significant amount depending on the home's value.

Homeowners Insurance

When purchasing a home through a lender, you will almost always be required to purchase homeowners insurance when completing the process. This will take care of any repairs or loss of belongings that are covered in the specific policy. When a complaint is filed against you for any accident, homeowners insurance will be needed, so it's extremely important to purchase the right amount to cover any problems you may face.

To recap, here are a few important tips regarding the home buying process. First, you must have enough money saved up to use as a down payment on your home. You must then find a loan with an affordable and low interest rate. Because you'll be paying thousands of dollars in interest over the lifetime of your loan, it's crucial to look for a low interest rate for the long term. Furthermore, you must be able to keep a strong credit score at all times for the most flexibility on your payments. Finally, you should be able to easily pay for closing costs and take that into account when searching for your next home.

Chapter 15
Insurance

The concept of insurance is a relatively advanced financial idea, but it has a pretty simple use: reduce risk. There are a lot of unknowns in the world. No matter how far society progresses, some things are impossible to avoid. Sometimes it's the environment, like a natural disaster occurring, other times it's other humans, from clumsy drivers to deranged criminals. While having savings is incredibly important to deal with unprecedented emergencies, oftentimes it isn't enough.

Buying insurance is a much safer and affordable way of financially protecting yourself from emergency situations than savings. Like a lot of things relating to personal finance, dealing with insurance is far from fun, but I can guarantee you it is important. Even though the words deductible and copay may sound like they are from another language to you, by the end of this chapter you'll have a firm understanding of different types of insurance as well as their importance.

What is Insurance?

Insurance is a form of financial protection that helps control risk and decrease loss. There are a lot of different terms related to insurance that you're going to have to understand before understanding how the system works as a whole. Although this might seem like we're dumping a bunch of vocabulary with no explanation (we kind of are), it will make more sense as you read further.

An agency that offers insurance is called an insurer. A person or organization that buys insurance is recognized as a policyholder. When insurance is bought, the policyholder is awarded a contract, known as an insurance policy, that specifies the terms and situations under which the insurer may pay the policyholder. The recurring payment that goes from the policyholder to the insurer in order to maintain this contract and protection is called the premium.

Your insurance kicks in when you file a claim that you or your possessions have endured damage; it is essentially activating the contract you purchased. If your claim meets the insurance policy's rules, then your insurance pays for replacing, repairing, or reimbursing the cost of the thing that was damaged. However, in most cases, the insurance won't pay the full amount of your first expense. Insurance providers expect you to pay what is called a deductible before they step in and cover the rest of the costs. Deductibles reset every time the contract resets, but the good news is that the money paid towards a deductible goes towards your emergency, and not the insurance company.

Health Insurance

Health insurance is a policy that ensures that you and your family can pay for necessary healthcare. We'll talk about this more in-depth in Chapter 16, but here is a brief overview. In a health insurance contract, the insurance provider is responsible for the cost of medical care for every family member. The insurer pays for all the costs related to a condition for which the covered person needs care, in return for a monthly premium.

Although private health insurance is the most common type in this category, the government does offer the following two public options.

I. *Medicare*

This public insurance plan primarily covers individuals over the age of 65, people with certain rare diseases, and younger individuals who meet select criteria. This functions essentially the same as private insurance, however, the premiums and deductibles tend to be significantly lower than for-profit insurance. Recently, there has been a push in the government to expand this kind of healthcare to all people in a plan called 'Medicare for All'. In the case that this goes through, the health insurance arena may look significantly different than it is now.

II. *Medicaid*
This form of healthcare is for low-income individuals who do not fall into Medicare eligibility, but cannot afford private insurance. Medicaid functions in a similar manner to Medicare, however, it offers some services like nursing and personal care that Medicare does not. As of now, the program is one of the largest in the U.S. serving 68.8 million people and spending a total of over $597 million in 2018 alone.

Health Accounts

A Health Savings Account, HSA, is a savings account that is used for personal and familial healthcare expenses. To be eligible to open this account, you must qualify for a High Deductible Health Plan, HDHP, which has a certain minimum deductible you must pay. This type of account lets you allocate money on a pre-tax basis to pay for medical expenses.

An HRA, or Health Reimbursement Arrangement, is similar to an HSA in that it is a health plan that helps reimburse individuals for out-of-pocket medical costs. However, an HRA is solely offered by an employer and is used to reimburse you for medical expenses and insurance premiums.

Liability Insurance

Liability insurance is used to cover property, vehicles, and corporations. The insurance provider will financially reimburse the owner in the event of any harm to property protected in the policy.

I. *Auto Insurance*
According to the Insurance Information Institute, the average loss on each auto claim is $4,900. That's a huge amount, making it critical to have insurance to not pay those costs. Your auto insurance can be covered through liability insurance, but this only covers minimal needs like injury from car crashes. Two other forms of insurance cover your other needs:
- Collision Coverage covers your car replacement or repairs after a crash.

- Comprehensive Coverage is not necessary, but it covers your car from natural disasters, vandalism, and theft.

II. *Property Insurance*

This insurance protects homeowners and renters against damage to real estate property. Common occurrences protected include floods, fires, theft, and natural disasters. For landlords, specifically, this insurance also covers tenant misuse.

III. *Corporate Liability Insurance*

Primarily, this insurance covers businesses' assets including transportation, real estate, and commercial properties and reimburses them when damages occur. Additionally, it covers customer issues that cost the business money and resources. For example, qualms concerning advertising, copyright, and slander against a business. Similarly, it also protects against other customer complaints or damages.

Life Insurance

Life insurance reimburses your family financially if you pass away early. You pay a regular premium to the insurance provider for a specific number of years and in return, if you pass away during the span of the policy, the insurance provider pays an amount promised to your family.

There are two main types of life insurance: term life and whole life.

I. *Term Life Insurance*

This form of insurance is set up for a certain amount of time. If you die within that allotted time, your close family will be able to withdraw money from the policy. In terms of pricing, it rises with a person's likelihood of dying during their lifetime and has no cash value after the term expires. If you get diagnosed with terminal cancer and try to purchase life insurance to easily get your family money, you will be greeted with extremely high premiums, since the likelihood of your death is high.

II. *Whole Life Insurance*

Whole life insurance, or permanent life insurance, lasts for your whole life. Premiums on this insurance tend to be more expensive than term insurance but are not subject to change over time like that of term insurance. The benefits of this asset come in cash and are transferred without taxes. Something else to note about this insurance is that it also covers burial expenses, which can be quite expensive in modern America, going into the tens of thousands.

Importance of Insurance

Insurance ensures stability and reduces the burden placed on you in times of unexpected circumstances. By obtaining protective insurance, you will allow your family to have a bright future. Remember that your insurance will vary and depend upon your economic and family circumstances. As your financial capital increases, your human capital usually decreases. Thus, it's important to purchase the right amount of insurance to keep you fully covered for any situations that you have to deal with in the future.

SECTION 5:
END GAME FINANCE

Although you can pretend that you will be the same nimble, quick-thinking person you are now when you hit old age, chances are you won't be. This means you'll eventually have to end your career and head into retirement. It might be tempting to think that the moment you hit 66, you'll be in Bora Bora, sitting on a hammock, drinking a martini in the sun, but the truth is that retirement can be a difficult experience if your financial habits and practices have been poor leading up to it.

The importance of managing your wealth both before and during retirement cannot be overstated. We mentioned to you before that as a teenager, you have a long life in front of you, and that means that the mistakes you make right now don't have that large of an impact on your life, since you have time to change them. Mistakes made in retirement aren't as forgiving. As the number of years left in your life decreases, recovering from poor financial decisions becomes more difficult. Thus, it is important to properly plan your retirement. In this section, we will be talking about more advanced forms of income generation, social security in America, concrete retirement plans, and the big bad topic of estate planning.

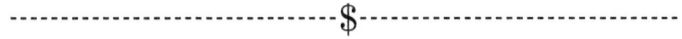

Chapter 16
Real Estate

Although we talked about investing in securities earlier, we're now going to explain how to invest in real estate properties. Real estate investment takes a lot more time and commitment than investing or trading stocks, since oftentimes you are dealing with a lot more capital, and have to interact with many people to buy, maintain, and sell real estate.

However, when done right, real estate investment offers so much more than just investing in securities. As opposed to the high volatility of the stock market, real estate investment has a more consistent appreciation of wealth. Additionally, rather than adding to the taxes you have to pay like securities, real estate investment can often give you deductions in taxes, helping you retain more of the wealth that you've earned. The primary reason people tend to wait later in life to invest in real estate is that it requires a level of financial stability and security, as well as saved up capital. Although debt financing is possible and almost always used in real estate, it's safer to minimize the obligations you have, which is why starting with a good base of capital is important.

Residential Properties

Residential properties include single-family homes, duplexes, and condominiums—basically any building that functions primarily as a living space. As these properties typically require less money up-front, they are best suited for investors new to the real estate market. Residential properties allow for simpler financing options and more straightforward management responsibilities when compared to other types of real estate. Over time, this allows for consistent and periodic income from rent, as well as appreciation in property value.

Commercial Properties

Commercial properties include office spaces, retail stores, industrial complexes, apartment complexes, and warehouses. These properties are much larger and more difficult to manage compared to residential properties. Many of these properties are also extremely expensive. However, the payoff tends to be much greater with a 13% annual average return compared to that of residential properties which typically only reach 9%.

Before you get any ideas about trying to own a whole commercial property by yourself, understand it's very time and effort-intensive, so dividing the purchase and the profits with investment groups is usually a better option. Compared to buying a second house to rent out, owning something like a strip mall is a significantly bigger commitment.

Online Resources

There are many online websites and applications that can be helpful in the real estate investing process. For commercial real estate resources, helpful websites include LoopNet.com and CREXi.com. These websites provide potential investors with the various types of commercial properties available in their desired area and will provide them with extensive details including sale type, Capitalization (CAP) rate, Net Operating Income (NOI), size, and realtor contact information. For residential purposes, you can use zillow.com and trulia.com. These websites allow investors to look at purchase history, square footage, and other necessary specifications.

Analyzing a Property

When analyzing a rental property, there are three main factors you must consider: the contextual location, the price and condition, and the CAP rate (commercial uses).

The most important factor to look at is the location for example you would want your business to be in a populated area or a housing property to be next to a school since they tend to attract buyers. The second factor you have to consider is the price and condition of your potential property. Oftentimes lower quality properties require repair and as such their prices are lower. It is in your best interest to see whether the condition of a building matches its price and if it is similar to that of other buildings in the area. The last and final thing to analyze when purchasing a property is the CAP rate or a statistical measure of the worth of a building. The formula for this indicator is the NOI divided by the market value of the asset. The higher the CAP rate, the better the commercial investment as it ensures you get your bang for your buck. Following these four rules will ensure you don't make a misguided purchase.

Real Estate Investment Trusts

A Real Estate Investment Trust (REIT) refers to when a business uses a pool of investors' funds to buy and manage real estate properties. Shares in these trusts are bought and sold and investors are able to make non-residential investments that aren't available for direct purchase. Think of them as the 'mutual fund' for real estate. Typically, investing in commercial real estate properties like office buildings, restaurants, and retail stores requires a lot of money and risk, but this method allows for it to be spread amongst numerous partners.

A Real Estate Investment Group (REIG) is almost the same thing as a REIT, except that it doesn't have to be as formally organized as REIG. These groups do not have to follow the same restrictions that REITs do, but they can still choose to buy, flip, or sell properties for an additional source of income.

Making Money

With all this said, the main goal of buying real estate is to get that dough, so what are the actual ways in which you make money? The two main methods of earning money through real estate are the following: asset appreciation and rental income.

I. *Appreciated Value*

Real estate prices rarely stay the same, as they fluctuate based on market factors, just like stocks do. Though, predicting whether real estate will appreciate or not is relatively easy. The context in which a property or piece of land is situated is the biggest factor in price. If the neighborhood is growing, with a lot of people moving in or starting businesses, then the market value of real estate around that area should increase as well. Similarly, established neighborhoods with good school districts and employment opportunities often see high appreciation in real estate value.

II. *Rental Income*

One of the biggest reasons people purchase properties is to generate an additional stream of income. While property takes time to appreciate, it can also generate money for you if you choose to rent out space. Renting out a house or building means that you are allowing other people to reside in or use your space, in exchange for money. Although you will often have to deal with issues like insurance and repairs on behalf of the tenant, renting out a house provides a great deal of financial stability. On the off chance, a tenant fails to pay for the property they usually assign a guarantor or person who pays on their behalf to continue using the property. Even when you choose to rent your property, you still have the ability to sell it for a profit, if the property value increases.

House Flipping

House flipping is a specific type of short-term real estate investment strategy that deals with purchasing and reselling houses in a short period of time. This minimizes the mortgage interest payments you must make and the insurance you must purchase, but also doesn't allow for a lot of appreciation for the property. However, the way house flippers add value to the property is by renovating the space. By buying a somewhat poorly maintained house for cheap, a house flipper can make repairs and restore the house to a better condition and sell it for a profit.

House flipping can be comparable to swing trading in the stock market. Both deal with an active income-generating strategy rather than a passive long-term investment. This means that you have to spend a good chunk of time and effort in order to increase the value and actually earn money, rather than sit back and wait.

Chapter 17
Social Security and Welfare

Although America is widely considered a capitalist country, the government provides a social welfare program for the unemployed and impoverished. The concept of social welfare, in general, is the collection of a percentage of income from all workers, to distribute to those in need. Certain requirements need to be met for someone to qualify for welfare benefits, but we'll talk about that more in detail later.

What is the American Social Program Sector?
For the past couple of decades, the American government has created and supported a government-supported financial safety net for millions of people. This includes a multitude of programs including social security, government-sponsored healthcare, and numerous other initiatives ranging from food stamps to education. These programs benefit about 68 million Americans annually, although that figure tends to increase during economic shocks, as more people who find themselves newly unemployed will qualify.

These programs can be divided into two easy-to-differentiate categories: means-tested and universal. Means-tested programs depend on your income for aid; most of the time you would have to be a lower-income individual to qualify. Universal includes programs such as social security which are open to everyone (but could still be proportional to income). If you ever have to navigate through the social safety net system make sure to note this difference.

As a side note, one thing we would like to note is the fact that the American welfare system tends to be rather inefficient. Oftentimes, specific programs, even universal ones, have lots of bureaucracy, paperwork, and steps to provide any aid, making it very difficult to take advantage of the system. Be prepared to deal with an arduous application process if you ever find yourself in a position where you are interacting with some of these government programs.

What is a Social Security Number?

A social security number (SSN) is a 9-digit number given to every United States citizen and permanent and working residents. The government uses this number in order to keep records of your income and timeline of employment. Your SSN is used to obtain credit, open bank accounts, obtain insurance coverage, and purchase a property or vehicle.

This is an example of a social security card.

Benefits

Social Security exists to provide a solid financial foundation for all Americans; as such, it brings a host of financial benefits. The four main ones are listed below.

I. *Retirement*

If you work for at least ten years, you could receive retirement benefits. This is based on your highest 40 years of earnings and is on average $1,450.

II. *Spousal*

Spousal benefits include possible eligibility for those who are married or have been for a minimum of ten years. If your retirement benefit is less than half of your spouse's retirement benefit, you could be eligible for a greater amount.

III. *Survivor*
At age 60, a survivor can legally collect their deceased spouse's retirement benefit. This may either begin immediately or after a couple of years, according to your specific information.

IV. *Disability*
This program assists individuals who are unable to get a job as a direct result of a health condition. Amounts provided vary, but it ranges from $800 to $1,800. In 2020, the average was $1,258 monthly.

Common Welfare Programs

I. *Temporary Assistance for Needy Families*
The Temporary Assistance for Needy Families (TANF) program is the widest-reaching welfare program in America, having supported over 422,000 adults and 1.6 million children in 2019 alone. Its primary purpose is to provide direct financial assistance in the form of liquid capital to struggling families. On average, benefits received from this program are about $480 per family. Since this amount is far below the necessity for many families, it is often employed in tandem with other programs.

II. *Supplemental Nutrition Assistance Program*
The Supplemental Nutrition Assistance Program (SNAP) is commonly referred to as food stamps. It provides 34 million Americans with access to subsidized food items. On average, each household receives about $246 per month.

III. *Housing Assistance Programs*
Although there is not a single federal program that does this, all programs share similar ideas and principles, which are regulated by the United States Department of Housing and Urban Development (HUD). The goal of these programs is to ensure that no family spends more than 30 percent of their household income

to pay for rent. As of December 2019, this program served 5.2 million households and over 10.4 million people by providing subsidized rent. This program is often used in tandem with the Low-Income Home Energy Assistance Program that provides families with subsidized energy and house insulation. Together, these programs work to create sufficient housing conditions and reduce the financial burden of keeping a roof over someone's head.

IV. *Earned Income Tax Credit*

The Earned Income Tax Credit (EITC) program supports families who make less than $52,000 annually by providing them with a tax return i.e. a 'tax credit' allowing for more financial flexibility. In 2018, this program worked to serve 22 million Americans and on average, it provided $3,191 in benefits for families in need.

Universal Program Future

While this system of welfare may seem complicated, there is a good chance it won't even apply to you in the future, the reason being, Universal Programs. These programs are welfare programs all Americans can access independent of wealth status and ones that do not require applications. An example includes former presidential candidate Andrew Yang's Universal Basic Income Plan that was meant to give each American $1,000 a year.

These programs are increasingly becoming more popularized in developed countries as they circumvent some of the common problems with welfare. Primarily, they ensure no American doesn't receive support; since welfare runs through so many different program channels, applications, and bureaucracies, millions of eligible Americans end up not getting care and those who do lose money from these arduous processes and end up getting support far too late. To work their way out of this program system, countries like the U.K. and even the state of Alaska implemented Universal Income Programs that created positive economic growth. With the current status quo of American poverty not changing, the advent of these programs is very likely in the future. Thus, keep weary of how these kinds of situations can affect you and your finances.

Chapter 18
Retirement and Savings Plans

Although in the previous section we talked about employment and how to get a job, once you reach the age of retirement, you need a steady stream of income to support you and your living expenses, without working. That's where retirement plans come in. Retirement planning applies to saving, investing, and safely distributing money to save up for retirement.

Saving for retirement isn't typically as simple as just putting away money in an account somewhere and breaking it out when you want to quit your job, but it can offer a lot more advantages than a basic savings program.

Qualified vs. Nonqualified Plans

Saving for retirement is something that is encouraged by the government, however, there is a big distinction between ones that are actually government 'endorsed' and ones that are not.

Qualified plans are signed off by the IRS and give employers and employees tax advantages if they meet certain criteria including having tax-deductible employer contributions as a business expense, employee contributions are made with pretax only, and interest earned on the contributions is tax-deferred to begin.

On the other hand, nonqualified plans do not have tax advantages and do not need to be approved by the IRS. These plans can show discrimination towards certain employees and cannot have tax-deductible contributions.

401(k) Plan

A 401(k) is a qualified taxable retirement plan sponsored by companies. It is established by the employer and gives a tax break to those employees who are saving for retirement purposes. Retirement plans incentivize people to plan for their future and save up, by giving tax breaks and a structured retirement.

Usually, there is an upper limit to the financial contributions one can make to any type of 401(k) plan. This is to mitigate the divide between high and low-earning individuals.

Roth vs. Traditional 401(k)

When it comes to the typical 401(k) retirement plan, there are two options: traditional and Roth. They differ from each other based on the way they are taxed. A traditional 401(k) plan takes income before taxes and puts it into the plan. When you withdraw though, you do have to pay the taxes. A Roth 401(k) works the other way: the income you save in the Roth plan is after paying taxes, however, during your retirement all withdrawals are tax-free.

Both of these types have their advantages and disadvantages, and you should weigh what priorities and expectations you have for your work and retirement life before starting either. Due to the United States's progressive income tax system, you will likely be in a lower tax bracket during your retirement, than when you are working. This is why many people advocate for the traditional 401(k).

Employee Stock Ownership Plan

An Employee Stock Ownership Plan (ESOP) is a company benefit plan, where employers receive and maintain a certain amount of stock, usually at below-market prices. This plan also provides the company, shareholders, and participants involved with tax benefits. After companies set up a trust fund for employees, they usually allocate money for purchasing the stock or privately send the shares to specific people. Staff members can either sell it directly on the market or return it to their employer.

What Happens if I Switch Companies?

It depends on the amount invested and your specific conditions. Firstly, consider how much money you have in your account. If it is less than $1,000 you cannot leave it with your employer. If you have between $1,000 and $5,000 your employer must help you set up an IRA, which we will discuss later, and if it is greater than $5,000 you can keep it with your employer. However, no matter the circumstances, you can rollover your 401(k) to your new employer or reinvest that money into an IRA account.

How to Invest Using Your 401(k) Savings

Before Investing in specific funds through a 401(k), you should look at two things: age and risk tolerance. Depending on your age, the amount of money you put in your 401k should be proportional. You may not be able to invest as much at a young age but hopefully, as your age and income rise, you can contribute more. To have a sufficient amount for retirement, you'll need a large principle. The second factor you will need to consider is how risky are you willing to go with your investments, we would recommend a moderate strategy between conservative investments and high-risk investments to optimize your risk to reward ratio. Afterward, you can choose an ETF or mutual fund you'd like and see it through. A good rule of thumb is to subtract your age from 100 and invest that percentage of your portfolio into stocks.

Individual Retirement Account

An Individual Retirement Account (IRA) is another type of retirement plan, except it is completed by yourself. You must open an IRA account with an institution that has been permitted by the IRS (ex. banks, credit unions, and brokerage companies).

Chapter 19
Estate Planning

No matter how many times you tell yourself that you will live forever, the truth is your time on earth is limited. When you pass, what will happen to your possessions and properties? On your way to the grave, you will still be bothered by the woes of estate planning, or the process of planning for how your wealth will be distributed after you die.

While we may not be able to help you with the whole death thing, we can do you an even bigger service and walk you through the steps of estate planning, the methods involved in it, and some extra information you will need to learn through this chapter.

Estates

As defined earlier, an estate consists of the assets of a deceased individual after their debts are paid off. Specifically, an estate regards anything that encompasses an individual's net worth including real estate properties, securities, stocks, bonds, bank accounts, vehicles, business interests, etc. Almost all personal debt has the same lifetime as the borrower and will not be passed along to other surviving family members. However, debts including loans and credit card balances are transferred and are then encompassed within the estate.

Transfer Methods

There are four primary ways in which you can transfer your estate to others. First, a will can be used to control property that may be probated. Next, you may choose to create a trust which will have a trust agreement that can control who is to receive the assets. Furthermore, a transfer on death or pay of death designation may transfer assets to a beneficiary. Lastly, a beneficiary designation, which can transfer an asset to someone else after the owner's death, can also be used.

There obviously has to be a legal process in which these methods must be conducted; this process is called probate. The probate process is used to determine the legitimacy and validity of wills and check if they will be executed. This process consists of appointing an executor, validating the will, allowing for challenges to the will, overseeing the distribution of assets, and filing the necessary reports for the process. This process will accrue various expenses for the legal, executor, and court purposes that can range anywhere between 1%-9% of the estate's value.

Wills

A will is a physical request for distributing your wealth. The people selected to receive a segment of your estate are called beneficiaries.

There are two main kinds of wills:
- A Simple Share will is designated for smaller-sized estates and designates the estate to be given to the individual's spouse.
- A Traditional Marital Share will is suited for larger-sized estates that provide half of the estate to the spouse and the other half to the designated children.

Trusts

A trust is a legal document transferring the assets to a named trustee who then manages the assets. This document is created by a person called a granter. There are many different kinds of trusts, but the most important include the living trust, revocable living trust, irrevocable living trust, and standard family trust. A living trust is when the trustee is assigned while living. A revocable trust is a trust that can be dissolved, and an irrevocable trust is something that cannot be changed. Lastly, a standard family trust is meant for children in one's family.

Non-Probate Process

I. *Transfer on Death*

Using this process, the ownership of assets is automatically transferred to a designated beneficiary in the event of the original owner's death. Stocks, bonds, and other investments are most commonly used in this kind of process.

II. *Beneficiary Designations*
This method is used to transfer holdings such as Roth IRAs and 401ks. Through minor legal paperwork, these assets can be automatically transferred to various networks.

Both of the above methods can conflict and circumvent wills; your will does not have the final say. Thus, when you are in this part of your life, it is important to make sure that overlap or potential grounds for conflicts are not present if you use a combination of transfer processes. Having these conflicts can lead to misallocation and depreciation of assets—avoiding them is critical.

Estate Shrinkage

This term refers to a decrease in an estate's value because of paying the creditor's claims, estate administration costs, and taxes, which are necessary to settle the estate. Your family will not get what they need for their assistance, or your beneficiaries may not get what you want them to have if your estate shrinks too much.

Power of Attorney

A Power of Attorney is a document that grants an individual the power to make legal decisions on behalf of the grantor or the person transferring ownership of a financial entity. This document is primarily used when the person isn't available to sign any legal document for a variety of financial reasons.

SECTION 6:
MISCELLANEOUS TOPICS

When you walk into the real world, there are many options that you will have career-wise, however, an alternative to the common workplace that more and more people are entering into is entrepreneurship. In this section, we want to take you through the process of launching your very own business and ultimately leave you with the confidence that you will be able to use it in order to succeed as an entrepreneur if that's what you choose to pursue.

However, on the grungy underside of both finance and entrepreneurship lay much worse ways to make a dollar: financial schemes. While you may think that you'll never be tricked into paying the alleged Nigerian Prince in your email inbox, schemes have gotten much sneakier and much more complex in recent years. We want to educate you on this issue, so you never fall victim to a 'multi-level marketing scheme' you see on Instagram or a 'Ponzi scheme' brought to your attention by your uncle. We hope you leave this section with a genuine and deep understanding of both these topics and can apply this knowledge in your own life.

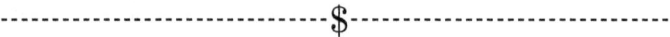

Chapter 20
Starting a Business

It can be extremely stressful to start a company. New entrepreneurs will almost always face countless problems from legal issues to product development to human resources, as well as so many more. Usually, new business owners are extremely confused and frustrated by all of the things they need to do to get a business running. For business owners, a smooth and successful launch can be backed by actually knowing all of the work involved in starting a business. Also, making smart decisions early can help guarantee growth. This chapter will help you accurately understand the steps needed to follow to start a successful and profitable business.

Outlined below is a step-by-step plan with the basics for starting a prosperous business.

1. *Think of an Idea*

    When brainstorming profitable and feasible business ideas, you will need to primarily determine what differentiates you from the rest of your competitors. Research similar existing businesses in your area and see if your proposed business idea will do something that they aren't.

2. *Perform Market Research and Create a Business Plan*

    After determining your provided product or service, you will need to conduct market research to see if there is a true need for your innovation. You will be able to learn about potential customers and compare those to your target customers and find competing companies in your market. You can then find a way to differentiate yourself from all other competitors and gauge an advantage. You will need to then write a business plan outlining your intended structure and the specifics of the operation. You may also need to brainstorm exit strategies for the future.

3. *Allocate the Necessary Financial Resources*

After creating your business plan, you will have a close estimate of the funds required to start your company. If you are not able to put in that money yourself, you will have to raise the capital from outside investors or take out a loan. You can also apply for business grants, which do not need to be paid back, or launch a crowdfunding campaign. Knowing a general estimate for the money needed to get your business running, will help you plan for the future of your company.

4. *Determine a Business Structure*

Various business structures are suited for different types of companies. For example, a sole proprietorship is suited for a business owned entirely by one person whereas a partnership is held by two or more people. A corporation is required if you want a different personal liability and company liability. You will have to determine the entity needed for not only the present but also the future.

5. *Choose the Business Location and Name*

You will need to determine a business name that accurately represents the brand's mission and make sure that it isn't already in use. After doing so, you will need to analyze who your target customer is and appropriately consider ideal locations to maximize customer traffic.

6. *Register Your Business and Apply for Licenses*

After you have decided on the specifics of your business, primarily the name, you will need to legally register it. This may be with the federal and state government, depending on whether or not it is affiliated with your personal name. To perform business and follow legal restraint, you will need to apply for licenses and permits. These will differ depending on your specific industry and operating location.

7. *Open a Bank Account and Purchase an Insurance Policy*

After you finish setting up your business, you should open a business checking account to store your revenue. This will allow you to differentiate your company and personal expenses. This will also help you to manage the cash flow of your business. After doing that, you need to buy an insurance policy because accidents such as fraud and consumer lawsuits can be expensive. Purchasing a policy will ensure that you are adequately insured.

By accurately completing all of the steps listed above, you will be able to get a successful and profitable business running. After completing this, you will need to focus on the day-to-day operations of your company including marketing, hiring staff members, finding manufacturers, and ultimately, growing your business. When promoting your business, you should write a unique selling proposition to show your customers why you are different and better than your respective competitors.

Chapter 21
Financial Blunders

With all we talked about throughout this book about building good financial habits, there are many ways to quickly destroy everything you have built. While the best thing to do to have financial stability is to maintain proper financial practices and build up your financial knowledge, you should also avoid the many pitfalls of finance.

There are many people out there in the world ready to exploit those who have limited knowledge in certain areas, which is a major reason we wanted to write this book. We want to ensure that you are equipped with the information needed so that you can't be taken advantage of.

As important as it is to know about these good financial practices, understanding financially exploitative practices can help you recognize the basic patterns of these blunders and avoid them.

Gambling and Lotteries

Although we talked about the uncanny similarities between speculative investing and gambling, straight-up gambling can be very destructive. Gambling is a highly addictive habit that can cause you great financial losses based on things that are completely out of your control. Gambling doesn't have to be limited to card games in ritzy casinos, however. Betting is a form of gambling that can get tied to any sport or game and can lead to massive losses. People usually get hooked on gambling after they win a decent-sized amount of money. While you may think that you'll stop once you win a certain amount, it's often incredibly difficult to stop until you literally have to, because you ran out of money.

Lotteries are also another financial trap. With seemingly low-risk, high-reward incentives, many lotteries hook people on the premise of getting rich quickly. The reality of lotteries, however, is that they often give you an astronomically low chance of winning, and a series of small purchases can add up really quickly.

With this being said, as long as it's legal and you aren't harming your current or future self by doing so, playing the occasional game of poker or buying a scratch-off ticket is not going to kill you. The biggest thing is having limits. Understanding that you won't make money from these and restricting the amount of money you spend on these activities can ensure that you won't ruin your financial life and regret your decisions later.

Financial Schemes

Since the creation of currency and financial instruments, there have been people willing to exploit those systems to take advantage of others. Although it might be easy to dismiss scams and cons as things that only the extremely gullible fall for, they are far more pervasive in society. Just to be clear, we're not telling you how these schemes work so that you can end up using them on unsuspecting people; we want you to be informed so that you can protect yourself against fraudulent actions.

I. *Ponzi Scheme*

The basic principle of a Ponzi scheme is to create a fake investment promising high returns within a short time period. The scammer first creates some kind of business or idea that he publicizes in order to draw investors' attention. They then promise an initial set of investors that the investment will generate a large amount of money. Since the investment isn't real, and it won't be able to generate any returns at all, the scammer finds another set of investors to buy into the idea. The money received from this second set is used to provide the initial investors with 'high returns'. While the investors from the second set believe that their money is going towards the actual idea, it is in fact being used to perpetrate the fraud. After they keep repeating this cycle of paying off previous investors with money from new ones, the scammer establishes enough credibility and receives enough capital to simply take all the money and abandon ship.

Now, you might be wondering, who is stupid enough to fall for something like that? Even for people with lots of wealth, it is easy to get enticed by the high returns often promised with Ponzi scheme investments. The main reason they do fall for these schemes is because of the fog of vagueness surrounding the investment. If the investors don't understand how it works, and the scammer sounds knowledgeable, then as an investor it would look like your money is in good hands.

The most common types of these schemes can fit into one of the following ideas: an overly complicated, 'advanced' security trading strategy, a 'revolutionary' piece of cutting-edge technology, or a business specializing in some obscure service. This combined with the exploitation of financially struggling people make this scheme especially deplorable.

II. *Pyramid Scheme*

A pyramid scheme is one of the most well-known financial scams, but it can still be easy to fall into. The idea of the pyramid scheme is that the scammer recruits people who recruit even more people below them. Each person typically has to pay some sort of an entry fee to participate in the scheme, but this fee is split between the top scammer and the actual recruiter. If they recruit more people, they get more money. The whole premise of the scheme, however, is typically built on some sort of mundane or menial task like sales of an educational course or product, that has no real value. Though, the actual sales don't matter, as recruiting is what gets the majority of the money.

III. *Affinity Fraud*

Affinity fraud encompasses all financial fraud that is done through the means of empathetic persuasion, where the fraudster either is in or pretends to be a part of a tight-knit social group and uses membership in that group as a means of tricking others in that group for financial gain. Groups can be religious, ethnic, political, or even familial.

IV. *Pump and Dump Scheme*

These schemes deal directly with investing in securities, most often penny stocks. Due to the highly volatile nature of penny stocks, and the low market capacity and circulation, they are subject to sudden changes in price. The pump and dump scheme involves artificially inflating the price of such a stock, typically through spreading false information online, to where investors begin rapidly buying up the stock. As a result, the stock's price starts rising. This is the 'pump' part of the scheme, where the prices are elevated. After the price increases by a considerable amount, the scammer sells all of his stock, the 'dump'. This leaves the victims who joined the scheme later on with a net loss.

Risky Investments

These kinds of investments promise very high returns in very high-risk enterprises. Examples of this include biotechnology firms with very high risks of failure, small-scale start-ups that require massive capital, and other kinds of industries that have not gone through much regulation. Ultimately, these kinds of investments may seem enticing, but when accounting for the risk they tend to have a higher chance of causing you to lose money. If you do find something particularly appealing in one of these businesses, make sure it only occupies a small portion of your portfolio; this ensures that even if the stock tanks, you don't suffer a tremendous loss. Doing so ensures that even in the worst-case scenario only a part of your invested wealth takes a hit.

Glossary

Section 1

Budget - A spending plan for a specific future period of time based on an individual's income and expenses.

Net Worth - The value of a person or organization's assets minus liabilities.

Section 2

Appreciation - A rise in the value of a specific asset over time.

Asset - A resource owned by an individual or organization that has financial value or is anticipated in the future to have value.

Asset Allocation - The mix of various financial assets among which an investor distributes their money.

Arbitrager - An individual who exploits inequities in currency conversion rates to turn a profit.

Bear Market - A market when stocks are decreasing in prices.

Blue-chip Stock - A type of stock that is from an established company and is considered to be a good investment.

Bonds - A form of investment that is essentially a loan to the bond issuer from the lender.

Book Value - The net value of a business's assets as per their balance sheet.

Broker - An individual who represents someone when buying or selling their assets.

Glossary

Brokerage - A firm that acts as a medium between stock exchanges and investors, handling transactions as a middleman.

Bull Market - A market when stocks are increasing in prices.

Capital Gain - The monetary gain that emerges from the sale of an asset that has risen in value.

Capital Loss - The loss incurred by an investor when they sell an asset that has depreciated in value.

Certificate of Deposit (CD) - A product offered by banks that provides individuals with an interest rate premium in exchange for an unmoved deposit.

Commodities - Raw commercial goods that can be used interchangeably with others of the same type without significant differences.

Company-Level Investment - An investment strategy that analyzes the intrinsic value of smaller assets and makes purchases independent of the overall market.

Contrarian Investment - An investment strategy consisting of buying assets in struggling portions of the market to profit from a rebound.

Depreciation - A decrease in the value of a specific asset over time.

Diversification - The spreading of investment into different investment instruments and asset groups to reduce risk.

Dividends - Payments that a corporation makes to share profits with all of the company's stockholders.

Equity - An individual's ownership in a certain asset or group of assets.

Exchange-Traded Fund (ETF) - A type of diversified fund that allows you to purchase multiple stocks and bonds in a single transaction.

Expense Ratio - A measure of mutual fund administrative and operating costs relative to assets.

Face Value - The explicit dollar value of financial instruments like stocks or bonds.

Fundamental Investment - An investment strategy based on market speculation or how others will soon react to a company's investment and financial statement.

Index Fund - A mutual fund composed of assets representing a market index.

Inflation - The decline of buying power over time for a specific currency.

Initial Public Offering (IPO) - The first time a business sells shares to investors in a large-scale quantity to the general public.

Investment Compounding - Reinvesting earnings from initial investment back into the investment.

Limit Order - A type of order used to purchase or sell a security if it hits a certain price.

Liquidity - A measure of how quickly an asset can be converted into cash.

Macro-Based Investment - An investment based on large sectors of the economy and industries.

Market Index - A speculative portfolio of investment holdings that represent a subset of the stock market.

Market Order - An order to buy or sell stock at the current market price.

Mutual Fund - An investment fund that pools money into a managed selection of stocks.

Options - Agreements between a securities buyer and seller that the buyer has the right to buy a lot of stock or asset if certain time and price conditions are met.

Penny Stocks - Stocks that are worth less than a dollar and are given out by small companies, which are typically highly volatile and risky.

Principal - The amount of money taken out on a loan.

Recession - A long period of declining economic activity marked by a drop in production and GDP across at least 2 quarters.

Registered Investment Adviser (RIA) - A person who is allowed to provide financial investment services to customers.

Return On Investment - A quantitative percentage metric of how effective an investment is taken by dividing the revenue/appreciation generated over the cost of the initial investment.

Savior Plan Investment - An investment strategy that includes taking over a failing company by purchasing the majority of it and making internal changes in hopes of corporate recovery.

Stock - An asset that provides you with partial ownership of a business.

Valuation - The dollar value of a certain business.

Volatility - A measure of how quickly the value of an asset, stock, or other holding changes in value.

Yield - The income returned on an investment, usually in the form of a percentage.

Section 3

Annual Percentage Rate (APR) - The annual interest rate on credit card debt that is owed to the credit card company.

Annual Percentage Yield - A measure of the rate of return on an investment which accounts for compounding interest.

Automated Teller Machine (ATM) - A digitized machine that allows you to withdraw and deposit cash using credit or debit cards.

Balance Sheet - A document that offers an overview of a company's financial standing the financial standing of a company to prospective investors by describing its assets, liabilities, and shareholder equity.

Bankruptcy - A legal process that provides an opportunity for an individual or corporation who can no longer afford their debts to be freed from the obligation to pay those debts.

Cashback - A feature that some credit cards have that returns a variable percent of their its usage back to the user as a reward.

Cash Flow - The net movement of money into or out of an individual, family, or corporation.

Checking Account - A general daily use bank account that can be used to make payments and deposit earnings.

Closing Date - A date that indicates the conclusion of a credit card billing period.

Collateral - An asset whose ownership is given to a lender to guarantee the repayment of a loan.

Glossary

Compound Interest - The interest on either a deposit or loan determined using the initial principal value and their accumulated interest.

Credit History - The overall general trend in an individual's personal credit, credit inquiries, and credit utilization.

Credit Report - An annual record from a credit bureau with all of your personal credit accounts and history.

Credit Score - A three-digit number calculated based on your credit history that represents your credibility as a borrower.

Default - The failure to pay back debts by a certain time.

Inquiry - The act of when a lender or creditor requests previous credit history.

Liabilities - Any money or financial instrument with monetary value that an individual owes to another individual or entity.

Money-Market Account - A type of savings account that requires higher opening and monthly balances that shares some features of a checking account, like checks and debit card usage.

Mortgage - A type of loan that you can take out to purchase a house, which has set payments throughout a predetermined period of time.

Net Income - The profitability of a company determined by deducting all expenses from the total revenue.

Repossession - The claiming of collateral by lenders in the case of default.

Revolving Credit - A credit account from which you can repeatedly borrow from and payback within the borrowing limit of the account.

Savings Account - A long-term account where money is deposited with a nominal interest rate intended to minimize spending by limiting the quantity and size of withdrawals.

Subsidized Loan - A student loan provided by the government for which there must be a need for financial aid; they do not accrue interest while attending school.

Unsubsidized Loan - A student loan provided by the government for which there need not be any need for financial aid; interest will be added to the loan continuously.

Section 4

1098 - A document used to report interest rates and external costs on an individual's mortgages.

1099 - A document used to report income from dividends, transfer payments, and self-employment.

Amortization - The method by which a loan with compounded interest is divided into equal payments over a period of time, with each payment consisting of both interest and principal payments.

Annuity - An insurance plan that offers a fixed sum of money paid to a beneficiary each year after an initial investment is provided.

Commission - The amount charged by a financial adviser for selling a product. The amount is provided by a services company.

Deductible - The out-of-pocket cost before your insurance coverage can be used.

Down Payment - A sum of money you pay upfront whenever you make a large purchase, like a house.

Escrow - An account to which taxes and insurance payments are periodically paid to, to avoid paying a large lump sum of money at the end of the year.

Health Savings Account (HSA) - An account allowing those with high deductible policies to have a tax- free account for medical spending.

Pre-Tax Contribution - An investment/deposit to a certain account that is untaxed.

Premium - The recurring payment to receive the rights to an insurance policy.

Refinancing - The process of paying off and replacing an old loan in exchange for a newer one with typically lower interest rates.

Tax Credit - A tax break that directly reduces the dollar amount of taxes owed.

Tax Deduction - A tax break that reduces the tax liability of an individual or company by reducing their taxable income.

Tax Exemption - A document that allows you to be free from government tax obligations.

Taxable Account - An investment portfolio that a brokerage provides allowing for investment into stocks, bonds, and other securities.

W-2 Form - A form completed by employers detailing employee wages and money withheld for social security.

W-4 Form - A form completed by an employee to inform the employer about current tax status.

W-9 Form - A form used to confirm a person's, typically a first-time employee's, tax information.

Section 5

401(k) - An employer-provided retirement in which a certain percentage of your annual salary is invested into a retirement account and employers match your contribution.

Beneficiary - The recipient of an account or asset, normally after the death of its initial owner.

Capitalization Rate (CAP) - A measure used to differentiate various real estate investments based on potential returns.

Collective Investment Fund (CIF) - A group of various pooled accounts that are administered by a bank or trust company.

Estate Planning - The process of planning for allocation of financial and nonfinancial possessions after you pass away.

Estate Shrinkage - A decrease in the value of an estate due to death-related costs after the owner passes.

Gross Income - The total amount of income earned by an individual before subtracting taxes and insurance costs.

Guarantor - A third party who, if the tenant is unable to pay rent, offers to pay the owner.

Individual Retirement Account (IRA) - A type of account that lets individuals set aside certain amounts of monthly wages for investment through employers or financial institutions; tax-free withdrawal after age 59.5.

Living Will - A document that details the wishes of a person regarding their future medical care in the event where informed consent is no longer possible.

Net Operating Income (NOI) - A calculation that is used to determine the profitability of a real estate investment.

Power of Attorney - A designation given to a person trusted to make important financial decisions on your behalf.

Real Estate Investment Trust (REIT) - A group or company that owns multiple real estate properties as investments allowing individual investors to pool money into the trust.

Rollover - The process of moving funds from one retirement account to another while avoiding taxes and penalty fees.

Social Security Number (SSN) - A nine-digit number provided by the U.S. government to all U.S. citizens.

Trust - A contractual arrangement in which one of the parties grants another party the right to own property for the benefit of a person, called the beneficiary.

Vesting - The act of providing or receiving a right to payment, asset, or benefit.

Section 6

Affinity Fraud - A blanket term encompassing fraud perpetrated by using social connections with people in order to scam them.

Ponzi Scheme - A form of fraud where old investors are paid high returns using the contributions of new investors.

Pump and Dump Scheme - A scheme to artificially raise the price of a highly volatile security so that the fraudster profits from the increase.

Pyramid Scheme - A type of Ponzi scheme formed by recruiting people who then recruit even more people into the scheme, with a small fee required for admittance.

About the Authors

Avaniko Asokkumar is a senior at Centennial High School. Aside from his interest in business and finance, he enjoys spending time playing the cello and piano, and playing soccer with his friends. After realizing the lack of formal education regarding personal finance present in the public education system, he was inspired to write this book to help educate other teenagers.

Sai Bommineni is a 17 year old originally from Dallas, Texas. Outside of exploring personal finance, he has many interests such as playing basketball, riding his bike, and playing video games. He hopes to leave readers with a deep knowledge of personal finance and a desire to learn more.

Rohit Chakka is currently a senior studying at Centennial High School. While not partaking in the realm of business, finance, and economics, he is often playing tennis, practicing a number of instruments, and watching basketball. He sincerely hopes that his passion for finance will be fruitful for not just himself, but others as well, and is thrilled to be sharing this book with you.

www.ingramcontent.com/pod-product-compliance
Lightning Source LLC
Chambersburg PA
CBHW070646220526
45466CB00001B/319